SOLVING YOUR DOG PROBLEMS

 W9-BKK-918

Also by Michael Tucker
Dog Training Made Easy
Dog Training: Step by Step

SOLVING YOUR DOG PROBLEMS

A practical handbook for owners and trainers

MICHAEL TUCKER

HOWELL
BOOK HOUSE
New York

Maxwell Macmillan Canada
Toronto

Maxwell Macmillan International
New York   Oxford   Singapore   Sydney

Copyright © 1987 by Michael Tucker

All rights reserved. No part of this book may be reproduced or transmitted in any form or by any means, electronic or mechanical, including photocopying, recording, or by any information storage and retrieval system, without permission in writing from the Publisher.

Howell Book House
Macmillan Publishing Company
866 Third Avenue
New York, NY 10022

Maxwell Macmillan Canada, Inc.
1200 Eglinton Avenue East
Suite 200
Don Mills, Ontario M3C 3N1

Macmillan Publishing Company is part of the Maxwell Communication Group of Companies.

Library of Congress Cataloging-in-Publication Data

Tucker, Michael.
    Solving your dog problems: a practical handbook for owners and trainers/Michael Tucker. — 1st pbk. ed.
        p.   cm.
    Includes index.
    ISBN 0–87605–739–3 (pbk.)
    1. Dogs—Training. 2. Dogs—Behavior. I. Title.
[SF431. T83 1992]
636.7'.088'7—dc20   91–28334
                                                                  CIP

Macmillan books are available at special discounts for bulk purchases for sales promotions, premiums, fund-raising, or educational use. For details, contact:

        Special Sales Director
        Macmillan Publishing Company
        866 Third Avenue
        New York, NY 10022

First Paperback Edition 1992
10 9 8 7 6 5 4 3 2 1

Printed in the United States of America

Cover design: Echidna Graphics, Surrey Hills, Vic., Australia
Cover photography: Malcolm Cross and Associates, Vic., Australia

Contents

Breeds shown in this book

Acknowledgements

I wish to express my most sincere thanks to Dr Hugh J. Wirth, AM, BVSc, FAVA, President, RSPCA Victoria, for his tremendous support in writing the Foreword for this book and for the continued appreciation shown in connection with the services I provide within my work.

My thanks also go to Dr Michael Righetti, BSc, BVSc, for his guidance on veterinary matters, to Dr Harry R. Corbett, BVSc, for his contribution in the area of abnormal canine behaviour, and to Senior Sergeant Paul J. Demos, Chief Instructor of the Victoria Police Dog Squad, for his advice on police dogs.

I shall always be most grateful to my wife Valerie and daughters Sharon and Alison, who gave so much of their time and care in helping me take all the photographs for this book, and to all those who kindly brought their dogs along to be photographed.

My gratitude is extended also to the countless dog-owners who, over the many years, have brought dogs to me for training, during which time I have been able to study their temperament, behaviour and working ability.

Lastly, but by no means least, my sincere thanks go to Dorothy Wellington, who not only encouraged me to write this book but kindly undertook to type the manuscript.

Note

Certain measurements in this book are expressed in the metric system. For converting to their US (customary) equivalents:

2.5 centimetres (cm) = 1 inch
(thus, 25 cm = 10 inches, 50 cm = 20 inches, etc.)
1 metre (m) = 39.37 inches
1 kilometre (km) = 1000 metres (.621 mile)
1 kilogram (kg) = 2.2 pounds

Foreword

In the Australian ethos the desire to own and care for horses and dogs predominates. Since the majority of Australians are urban dwellers, ownership of horses is both impractical and financially impossible, so it should be of no surprise that of all the various types of pets available to be kept, dogs are by far the most popular and numerous.

Much has been written and said about the rewards associated with owning a dog. The almost total dependence of dogs on people for their health and general well-being is an endearing attribute which underpins the human–dog bond. And yet it is this very quality which, if not managed correctly, can make the ownership of a dog a most unpleasant experience.

There are two forces at work within the Australian community which influence the way we own dogs and can make ownership difficult. Firstly, although Australians are currently breeding and owning more dogs than ever before, most of us have little knowledge of the husbandry of dogs. The desire to own a dog, for whatever reason, is a powerful emotion that can completely override our ignorance of the necessity to select a dog on proven criteria — those that match type of dog to human personality, financial means, and other practical considerations. Secondly, the demands of modern urban living have made governments ultrasensitive to real or perceived nuisance factors. The need to appease ratepayers has already resulted in some harsh dog-control laws, with the threat of more draconian measures to come, and this can exacerbate some existing dog behavioural problems while helping to create difficulties that did not exist in former times. It is little wonder that in the past decade dog behavioural problems have become routine consultation cases for practising veterinary surgeons, and a major reason why dogs are abandoned to become another statistic at the local animal-welfare shelter.

Solving Your Dog Problems, the companion volume to *Dog Training Made Easy*, is a practical guide to solving behavioural problems and is written in a commonsense style that dispels much of the mystique and nonsense often associated with the subject. Michael Tucker has had long and varied experience as a dog-trainer, and has fully earned his reputation as a professional of high integrity. To be able to refer difficult behavioural cases to an expert who will quickly assess the problem, provide a straightforward prognosis and prescribe corrective training schedules if necessary, has been of immense help to my colleagues and myself for many years.

Solving Your Dog Problems will share this knowledge and practical advice with the wider dog-owning community.

I commend this book to all dog-lovers, and on behalf of those who cannot speak for themselves I hope that within these pages will be found wisdom and understanding.

Dr Hugh J. Wirth,
AM, BVSc, FAVA
President, RSPCA Victoria

Introduction

Since I wrote *Dog Training Made Easy*, which is for the average dog owner who needs to know the easy, step-by-step method of training a dog, I have become increasingly aware of the many and various problems people have with their dogs. In this book, I devoted a chapter to problems, but now I believe it is time to produce a book specifically covering the subject. I have received many requests to write such a book and although there are a number of books available on training dogs, there are very few which deal specifically with problems people have with their dogs.

And so I decided to do just that, and in a very simple way so everyone can understand. I endeavour to deal with as many problems as I can. While most are very common, others are only occasionally experienced. To really bring all these problems to life, I use many accounts of cases I have dealt with within my work, especially over the last 10 years. I explain the definite or likely causes of these numerous problems; how they developed and possibly become worse; how and if they can be corrected or controlled; and, what is even more important, how such faults can be prevented in the first place. This will naturally save many dog owners a lot of hard work and worry in months to come and will also ensure that both owners and dogs are able to live together in the greatest harmony imaginable.

In my daily work as a professional dog trainer, at least 50 per cent of my clients have major problems with their dogs. These dogs are brought to me because I specialise in dealing with problem dogs. But, I am happy to say, the rest of my clients do not really have any problems and just wish to learn how to train their dogs properly so that nothing goes wrong. A very sensible approach, which I highly commend. I also find that whenever I am invited to hold special dog training courses, usually for dog training clubs throughout Australian states or overseas, I meet up with quite a number of problems in canine behaviour, numerous undesirable temperamental traits in dogs and many faults in the training of both owners and dogs.

Most problems are caused initially by sheer ignorance on the part of the owners, most of whom are ready to admit it. Countless times clients have confessed to me, 'I realise now that I'm the problem, not so much my dog! I've caused it and the dog's been the one who's suffered, poor old dog. Now I realise that I've got much more to learn than my dog in the training lessons!' Yes, what they openly admit to is perfectly true. Unfortunate as it is, it is nearly always the owner's fault. Problems are not always caused by something they have done wrong, but sometimes by something which they have not done but should have.

There are cases from time to time, and always will be I guess, where the problems have not been caused by the owners, but by other people or by some unfortunate circumstances. In some of these cases, I place the blame on breeders for breeding from stock with undesirable temperaments or rearing puppies in poor conditions and bad environments. In other cases, problems have appeared when dogs have arrived home after being boarded for a time in kennels where they have been mistreated in some way. I have also seen a few cases of bad temper-ament which have been the result of particular internal troubles the dogs have had. Until such times that the troubles caused problems, the dogs appeared to be perfectly fit to both their owners and veterinarians. Thankfully these cases are rare.

Perhaps the biggest problem in society today is the over-population of dogs. It would not be so bad if all owners looked after their dogs prop-erly, but regrettably a lot do not. There are vast numbers of unwanted dogs which are either allowed to stray or, worse still, get dumped by the own-ers. They end up in local pounds and various animal shelters. It is all a very sad business, and those dogs not claimed or found new homes within a certain time have to be painlessly destroyed. These figures run into thousands every week.

Hopefully, some government leg-islation will be passed which will help control this over-population of dogs. I believe there should be a wider edu-cation program to guide people into the way of responsible dog owner-ship, and I further believe that such a program should start in schools.

It is good to see that there is an ever increasing number of obedience dog training clubs springing up in towns and cities. Great credit and appreciation must go particularly to the instructors, who give their spare time to conduct obedience classes for people in the community who want to do the best for their dogs. Some of the clubs may not have the expertise that others have, but they are at least all striving for the same goal — that of teaching people how to train their pets.

While these clubs do a wonderful job in helping people to have happy, well-behaved pets, I am very concerned and strongly opposed to the unscrupulous individuals and groups who try to teach protection work, whereby dogs are taught to attack. In the wrong hands this can be an extremely dangerous practice and the methods used are often callous and cruel.

Training a dog to do police dog work is a highly specialised job indeed. So highly specialised in fact that it should be confined to government-controlled police forces and armed services only, in which both men and dogs are specially selected and carefully trained. The police dog is used to effect an arrest only as a last resort, and the handler is held responsible for the use of the dog. Such a situation could be where an offender, armed with a weapon, resists arrest.

I feel very sorry for those owners who have taken their dogs to such groups for so-called protection work, man-work or whatever, and are lured into believing that everything will be all right. Most of them regret ever having attended such training when they realise their dogs have become unreliable, untrustworthy and positively dangerous. Owning such a dog is like having a loaded gun. I therefore do my utmost to persuade people not to indulge in any way in this type of training.

Throughout my life I have always found it a great privilege to share in the lives of other people by being able to help them in some way or another, no matter how great or small. In particular, when I have been able to train or give them advice in connection with their dogs, which I know means so much to them. So in writing this book I hope I will be able to reach out to and help countless more dog owners, not only in my home country, but overseas. I sincerely hope that what I have written will not only make them more aware of the numerous problems which they have with their dogs, but that they will gain a greater knowledge and understanding of how to deal with them and, most important of all, how to prevent even the smallest of faults developing. It is often the small faults which, if allowed to go unchecked, can eventually develop into major problems.

1 The First Lesson

Every week I receive a great number of telephone calls from dog owners who are seeking help and advice in training their dogs. While a few of them have no real difficulties with their pets, but just want to attend training lessons to teach their dogs the right way, most have problems in some form or another. Some are very common, others are not.

The common problems include pulling on the leash, jumping up at people, barking excessively through the day, mouthing their owner's hands (which often leads to biting later on), not coming when called, pulling the washing off the line, digging holes in the garden and generally being out of control! Problems which are not so common can include not wishing to go out for a walk on the leash, objecting to being groomed, having a dislike for certain people, being afraid of travelling in a car, not remaining in the stand position in the show ring and quite a few others.

First I write down the general information like the owner's name, address and telephone number, and the dog's pet name, breed, sex, age and the main problems, if any, which exist. I then go on to ask a few simple questions about the dog, like: 'How long have you had the dog? Can you recollect when the problem started and, if possible, how it started? What have you done to try to correct it? Is the dog taken out for a walk every day? Does the dog live outside all the time, or does it live inside the house with the family? Has the dog attended any dog training classes before? From where did you get the dog? Have you ever had a dog before? And, as a matter of interest, how did you come to choose a dog of that particular breed?' After this, most callers really seem to open up and tell me even more about their dog. By patiently listening, I can gain a pretty good idea about the entire problem, when it started, how it developed, what promoted it, and so on.

Take one such call as an example. A gentleman phones and explains: 'We have a 6-month-old German Shepherd male which we bought at 7 weeks of age. He has continually mouthed us since we have had him, although the breeder assured us that he would soon grow out of it. He is outside all the time, we cannot trust him in the house. He has recently taken to pulling the washing off the line and has now started barking excessively while we are out, which is annoying our neighbours who have naturally complained of the noise. Can you please help us, or is it too late to train this out of him?' Naturally, I always say that I will try, and that I will get a much better idea of the dog's temperament when I see him and how his owner handles him. So an appointment is made.

When they arrive by car at my training school I gain much by watching the owner pull up and get his dog out of the car. All too often I see the dog jumping around in the car and sometimes crying and barking in excitement. Then the dog forces its way out of the car as the door is opened, nearly knocking or pulling the owner over! The dog then pulls extremely hard on the leash as it tries to charge up the drive with the owner hanging on to the other end of the leash with all his or her strength!

Seeing this, it is perfectly obvious that the dog has no respect for its owner. It is highly excited and has a tremendous amount of excess mental energy. This has been brought about by the dog not being taken out enough and not receiving any training which would have helped it use up much of that excess energy.

While the dog might have a strong leather leash about 120cm (4ft) long, often it is only wearing a fixed leather collar with a buckle on it. I point out that in order to correct the dog effectively with a sharp jerk on the leash,

Fig. 1. How to thread up a slip-chain collar.

it should wear an appropriate slip-chain collar, preferably one with large long links. I produce such a collar, explain and demonstrate as to how it is made up (**Fig. 1**), the correct way it should go on when the dog is on the owner's left, and how it loosens itself as soon as the leash is slackened immediately after a corrective jerk has been given (**Fig. 2**). The incorrect way of putting the slip-chain collar on the dog is also shown, and it is explained why it will not loosen when the leash is relaxed (**Fig. 3**).

It is surprising the number of people who, when they get a dog, go to the local supermarket or pet shop and buy a cheap slip-chain collar which is far too long and a leash which is often made of chain with a leather handle

Fig. 2. The correct way of putting on a slip-chain collar. Note that the fine links come from the ring attached to the leash, through the other ring, and continue *over* the top of the dog's neck so that the collar loosens itself automatically when the leash is relaxed.

Fig. 3. The incorrect way of putting on a slip-chain collar. The fine links are going through the ring and underneath the dog's neck. In this case the collar will not loosen itself when the leash is relaxed.

grip. Equipment which is cheap in price is often cheap in quality. It looks nice and shiny, and ideal for the dog. But little do some people realise that, being of inferior quality, it is likely to break as soon as an effective corrective jerk is given to their large strong dog. I always advise people who need slip-chain collars to buy good strong ones. Anything which is made in Germany or Great Britain is generally of very good quality, possibly because both are dog training nations. Thus the quality of the equipment sold in those countries must be ideal, otherwise there would not be a market for it.

A few years ago a client came with her dog for training, and the slip-chain collar appeared to be all right. Up until this time the dog had received no training. Soon after I started training, I gave the dog a backward corrective jerk for pulling, and the collar snapped. The welding was no good at all. Fortunately the dog did not run off, but stood there. I was able to put the leash round its neck by passing the clip end through the handle of the leash, forming a noose to secure the dog until I walked it back to my house and put a more suitable and reliable slip-chain collar on it. This has made me very careful, and nowadays I inspect every collar on any dog which comes for training. If I do not think it is of a good quality, I draw the owner's attention to this and promptly put on one of my own slip-chain collars. The danger, of course, is that if the collar does break the dog might run off into the road and cause an accident and possibly get injured or even killed. So when you buy a slip-chain collar, it is best to go to a pet shop which deals with a good range of this type of equipment, and always be prepared to buy one of the more expensive types.

With regard to the ideal length and type of slip-chain collar you need, a lot depends on the size of your dog. I personally advise that for a very large dog, especially a dog which has a longish or medium-long coat, the slip-chain collar should have very long links (about 4 to 5cm long). Such links are very strong, are very effective when used properly, and do not cut into the dog's neck as the fine-link collars tend to do (**Fig. 4**). They release very well, and are often termed fur savers! This is because they do not cut the fur down the right-hand side of the dog's neck as much as the finer-link collars. When the fine links run through the round ring the fur gets in between these and the ring and, like a pair of scissors, cuts the fur. If the dog has had a lot of jerks, it is more likely to lose more fur.

When you jerk a dog, it should be done effectively. I always believe dogs should receive the minimum number of jerks possible for two reasons. Firstly, you want to get the best results in the minimum possible time, and secondly, it saves fur! Dogs which receive a lot of jerks in a very half-hearted manner over a period of time gradually build up such a resistance to jerks that finally not even a good solid jerk will have any effect. Thus jerks should be kept to a minimum and given effectively at the right time, the right height, the right angle and

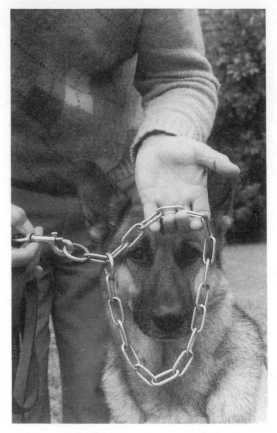

Fig. 4. The large-link slip-chain collar is better on medium to large dogs than the fine-link slip-chain collar. It is more effective, does not cut into the dog's neck, does not shave the semi- to long-coated dogs' fur on the right side of the neck, and is often stronger.

the leash should be quickly relaxed.

With regard to using a chain leash for training, this is most unwise as it can make your hands very, very sore and you cannot grip it as effectively as a leather leash. I always suggest that every handler gets a solid leather leash, at least 120cm (4ft) long, with a good snap hook on it, either hand stitched or with at least two rivets on each end of the leash. If it is much longer than 1.2m, it does become rather cumber-

Fig. 5. How to walk a dog freely on a slack leash.

Fig. 6. The safest and most effective way of holding a leash. (a) Put the palm of your hand through the handle of the leash, and (b) clasp your fingers and thumb around it.

some. If it is shorter than 1m, you will end up with other problems such as the dog or puppy becoming suspicious of things because of its limited area of independence, becoming protective because it is so close to the handler or becoming a puller because the leash is so short it becomes tight. And in training a dog to stay, you would not be able to to get very far away on a 1m or less length of leash.

When getting acquainted with a new dog, especially an excitable or timid type, I find it best to take the dog for a casual walk on the full length of the leash, allowing it to walk freely around me (**Fig. 5**). It does not matter in which hand the leash is held. It can be held in the left hand when the dog is on the left, or in the right hand when it is on the right. I also show the owner the safest and most effective way of holding the handle of the leash, which is for the palm of the hand only to pass through the loop, with fingers and thumb wrapped round it (**Fig. 6**).

I strongly advise people not to put the handle of the leash over their wrists (**Fig. 7**). I have seen so many accidents happen when handlers have held leashes in this way. One man was

5

Fig. 7. It is most unwise to put your wrist through the handle of a leash. This can lead to various accidents.

Fig. 8. It is dangerous to put your thumb through the handle of a leash. A sudden and unexpected quick pull on the leash could damage your thumb.

pulled over by his 90kg (200lb) St Bernard dog and dragged face downwards across a loose gravel road. I have seen a girl get accidentally bitten when her dog was attacked by another. It all happened so quickly. They whirled around as they fought, got tied up with the leash and, because she could not release it, her arm got in the way of one of the dog's jaws. I have seen numerous wrenched wrists and people pulled into the sides of doorways or other obstacles. So as a lesson in accident prevention, hold the leash securely, but also hold it so that you can release it immediately if necessary.

I also warn people against putting their thumbs through the handle (**Fig. 8**). This could easily result in thumb damage. Likewise with holding the handle over their fingers (**Fig. 9**).

For the first 5 minutes I take the leash and show the owner, who walks beside me, how to control the dog. I allow the dog to relax and do as it likes within reason. This means to walk along casually, look at things, have a little sniff and so on. I quickly point out that it is not within reason for it to charge off in any direction, pull excessively at any time, jump up at us or other people, chase after the local cat, bark at other dogs which may be in the street or anything else like that.

Usually within a second or two of starting, the dog pulls. I give a drawn out command, 'Steady', in a quiet, calm voice, quickly give a very firm backward jerk on the leash and immediately relax it (**Fig. 10**). The dog hears the command, gets a sudden shock from the jerk and responds by ceasing to pull. As soon as the dog responds like this I praise it vocally, 'Good boy!', in a quiet, slow manner, so as not to excite it. This correction and praise is repeated every time the dog pulls and commits any action I do not want. It is advisable to walk slowly, because if you walk fast, you will tend to excite the dog, and that is not what you want. You have to aim at keeping a slack leash and hold it high enough so that the dog can at least revolve around under the leash without getting its legs entangled in the leash. This does happen if you hold the leash down too low to the ground.

I then hand the leash over to the owner and show him or her how to give a command and the necessary physical correction on the leash. It is

Fig. 9. Holding a leash with one or two fingers is not only dangerous but insecure. Many a dog has broken loose from its handler when held this way.

Fig. 10. To correct the dog for pulling hard during free walking, give a quiet calm command, 'Steady', jerk backwards quickly and immediately relax the leash. When jerking have one foot straight forward and have all your body weight on your other foot. Use your body weight, and do not rely totally on muscle power.

not long before the dog responds equally as well for its owner as it did for me. Once shown, people soon develop the knack of giving this correction. By the following week, when they come for their second lesson, they are simply overwhelmed and say what a pleasure it is to be able to go for a walk with their dog and not to have it pull them along as had been the case before. Such behaviour had begun to make them dislike taking the dog out for its daily exercise.

Taking a dog for a short stroll like this is, I believe, time well spent, because it gives it time to get to know me as I am studying it, before I come to teach basic heelwork.

Holding the leash handle in my right hand plus one other point down the leash, also in my right hand, I position my hand in the centre of my body just below my waist so that what leash I have between my right hand and the dog hangs down in a U shape (**Fig. 11**). You should not hold the leash with your left hand, because if you do you are quite likely to put a little bit of tension on it. When the dog feels this, its natural reaction is to pull against the leash and thus promote the pulling problem. So start as you mean to go on — keep your left hand off the leash and only use it when you have to give a correction. Having adopted this stance, I am now in a position to start heeling the dog.

I give the command in an inviting way, 'Kim, heel!', and then step forward. The dog, wanting to accompany me, responds by taking its first step and as soon as I see its paw step forward, I praise it sincerely and immediately, 'Good dog!'.

Fig. 11. How to hold a leash when heeling your dog. Hold the handle of the leash in your right hand, plus one other point down the leash. Keep your right hand in the centre of your body below your waist line, so that the rest of the leash hangs down in a U shape.

Within the next few metres, the dog is likely to pull forward or even just start to lead ahead. As soon as this happens, I take hold of the leash, near the clip end, with my left hand (thumb on top of the leash), say in a quick, firm tone, 'Heel!', bend down to the dog's shoulder height, quickly and firmly jerk the dog back to my side, let go, stand up and stand quite still (**Figs 12 and 13**). At this point I have in effect chopped it right off! This is

Fig. 12. To correct your dog when it goes too far forward in heelwork, immediately take hold of the leash near the clip, with your thumb on the top, give a firm command 'Heel', and give a quick *horizontal* backward jerk.

Fig. 13. The instant you have jerked the dog back to your side, let go of the leash with the left hand, stand up and keep quite still for a few seconds before inviting the dog to 'heel' forwards again.

as much as to say, 'Now look here Kim, you are not going to take me for a walk. You wait there until I command you to heel at my side'. In a very short time the dog will get to know that it has to heel and not have its own way. I stand there for a few seconds, quietly command 'Heel' in an inviting tone, step forward at a moderate pace and praise it as soon as it responds. If, while I am standing there, the dog attempts to proceed forward, I stand my ground and jerk

it back again, as much as to say, 'I've not told you to move. You stay there until I say "Heel" and then step forward'. When you jerk a dog back into the heel position, it does not matter whether it sits or stands beside you. The important thing is that its head is beside you, and level with the front of your knee. It does not matter which foot you start off with, the main point is that the dog obeys you as you step forward.

The most important point you

Fig. 14. Having made the decision to sit your dog (at a kerb in this case), prepare your hands and leash a few steps beforehand.

achieve in this correction is that you get the dog to respect you. I am very particular about this, because on this hangs all your heelwork and indeed all the exercises you are going to teach your dog in the future.

Over the years I have had many people who have even been going to dog training clubs, and yet have difficulty with some of the more advanced exercises. I always ask them what their heelwork is like, to which they reply, 'Oh! No trouble at all'. So I give them about 1 minute of heelwork which includes a couple of turns and stops. And in that short time I see the cause of the problem, namely, the dog does not heel as well as it should, it leads out too much, goes slightly wide on the turns and does not sit immediately and straight when the owner comes to a halt. In other

words, the dog does not fully respect the owner. It is as simple as that. Therefore, is it any wonder that the owner is having a problem with a more advanced exercise like the recall for instance? So it is a case of getting that respect in heelwork first, and once this has been established other problems in other exercises are much easier to solve.

Finally, I come to the 'sit' in the heeling exercise. In addition to the two parts of the leash which I have in my right hand, I pass the clip part of the leash also into my right hand, while I am walking along with the dog at heel. At the same time I position my left hand, with the thumb facing to the left, over the dog's hindquarters (**Fig. 14**), give the command 'Sit', pull the leash up vertically above the dog's head with my right hand, pushing the

Fig. 15. To sit a dog, command 'Sit', hold the leash up vertically above the dog's head with the right hand and push the dog's hindquarters down and slightly forwards with the left hand as you stop with your feet together and straight.

dog's hindquarters down and slightly forwards with my left hand, and come to a stop with my feet together and straight (**Fig. 15**). As soon as the dog responds I slacken the leash and praise the dog vocally and physically with my left hand using very slow and gentle strokes on its head in order to keep it calm (**Fig. 16**).

The owner now takes over and is shown how to do the heelwork. It is interesting to note that after walking for about 100m (110yd) every owner remarks, 'It's amazing. My dog certainly seems to know what to do, especially when you were training him. I quite understand that I am the one who needs the training, my dog learns very quickly!' I always welcome it when people say these things rather than me tell them, because it really shows that they fully appreciate what they have to do in playing their parts in being responsible dog owners.

When a dog has been trained for several minutes, it must always be allowed to relax by being told to 'Go free', or words to that effect, with an explicit signal so that it understands that the work is finished for the time being until commanded to heel again. It is surprising the number of people who don't do this. Just imagine, if the dog is not dismissed from training, how will it ever know when it has finished? Just put yourself in this position. Would you know if you were not told? Take our everyday lives: ask a child at school, 'How do you know when you can go out and play' and he or she will say, 'When the teacher says so.' Or how do factory workers

Fig. 16. As soon as the dog sits, quietly praise it and give it slow gentle strokes to keep it calm.

know when they can finish work? When the hooter goes! Or, when are office workers allowed to go home? Yes, when it is 5 pm! Whatever your occupation, you have some means of knowing when you can finish work, and this must apply to dogs also. Simple, isn't it?

At the end of a dog's first lesson I advise the owner to practise a little every day. At this early stage the dog only needs about 10 minutes' training in a half-hour's walk and then it can walk freely on the leash for the rest of the time. But, if you have to cross over a road during that time, then bring the dog to heel and sit it at the kerb, heel it across the road, sit it on the footpath, praise it and tell it to walk free again. This does not take long and the dog learns that it must always cross over roads at heel.

Very often during the lesson a young dog will start to mouth my hands or those of the owner (**Fig. 17**), whereupon I show the owner how this must be corrected. The dog is given a firm word of reproof like 'No' or 'Leave', followed immediately with either an upward jerk on the leash or by taking hold of it by the scruff of its neck, with both hands, and giving it a couple of quick, firm shakes (**Fig. 18**). Provided you do this firmly, the dog should respond and respect you. The dog responds instinctively to this type of physical correction, because if it ever misbehaved when it was a puppy, its mother would pick it up by the scruff of the neck in her mouth, give it a severe quick shake and make it squeal, then put it down. The result was that it never ran away in fear or challenged her, but instead would re-

Fig. 17. Mouthing is an expression of the dog wanting to have its own way. This must be corrected immediately.

Fig. 18. Take hold of the dog by the scruff of its neck with both hands, say 'No' or 'Leave', and give it a couple of quick firm upward jerks and let go.

spect her. So if you do the same you should get the same results, and your dog will never hold it against you. Unfortunately, most people do not know of this type of correction, but instead hit their dogs with their hands, or a rolled up newspaper or stick. This is one of the worst things they can do, because they may make the dog afraid to the extent that it will run away to hide, especially if it is of a timid nature, or, if the dog is of a bold nature, it might take one or two whacks then retaliate and attack, not only the person who hit it but others as well.

I have seen some dreadful cases of dogs having been beaten, and such cruel acts are brought about, I believe, by sheer and utter ignorance on the part of the owners. Instructors at one local dog club told me of a case they had when a woman came to their club with her dog for the first time. When she lined up in the beginner class she was seen with a rolled up newspaper in her hand. The class instructor told her that they did not allow that means of correcting a dog, whereupon she actually had the nerve to admit that she had a metal rod inside it! She was promptly told not to use it again and was duly shown the proper way of giving a dog a correction on the leash.

While dogs mouthing people's hands is a natural act in most puppies, it amazes me when I hear breeders say to those who buy puppies from them, 'Oh! Your puppy will soon grow out of mouthing!' There is very little chance that they will stop unless they are corrected. In fact, it is quite likely to get worse and become a habit, a very bad habit, and one not to be tolerated. You see, if you allow that sort of thing to go on you are allowing your dog to have its own way and therefore it will not have that essential respect for you. If mouthing is not nipped in the bud at an early puppy age, it can get worse, even to the extent of a dog biting someone when it wants its own way. So remember, correct it as soon as it starts.

During a first obedience lesson many questions are asked which usually concern the dog's behaviour at home. These include barking and howling outside, digging holes, pulling washing off the line, climbing on to furniture in the home and jumping up at visitors when they arrive. I will discuss each of these in turn.

The most common cause of dogs barking and howling is because they are bored and frustrated. You often see this when the dogs are kept outside and not allowed to come into the house, and are never taken out for walks.

I get many telephone enquiries about this and my advice is to have the dog in the house, let it share life with you, let it meet your friends, take it out at least once a day, let it see the world, and let it meet other people and dogs in the park. 'Oh! I never really thought about that,' the caller replies. 'Will that stop him barking?' 'Well, let's put it this way', I explain, 'You've first of all got to get to the cause. It's quite plain the dog is lonely, bored and frustrated. How would you like it if you were shut up in a backyard day after day, week after week?'. There is a moment's silence and then the caller admits, 'Er! Well! No, I'm sure I wouldn't like it'. 'Well, try what I've just advised and let me know how you get on. It's true, the dog may need some training, but try that first!' Within a few days people phone back saying that the barking has stopped, the dog likes going out for its walks and the whole family really enjoy having it inside the house after all. They have all noticed that since they have made all the changes, the dog is so much more relaxed.

Dogs which pull the washing off the line, dig holes and pull up plants, etc., are usually dogs with high degrees of initiative and they want something to do. Once again, they should be taken out every day and given training which helps to use up some of their excess mental energy. It is also an excellent idea to see that dogs have plenty of toys of their own to play with, particularly when they are puppies (Fig. 19). But having taken all those precautions some dogs still carry out these naughty acts. Obviously the best thing to do is to catch the dog in the act, take hold of it, say 'No' firmly and give it a shake. It is no good doing this sometime after the event, you have actually got to do it the moment the dog goes for the

Fig. 19. Most dogs like to play with toys of their own and this helps to relieve boredom.

washing or goes to dig a hole. If you cannot be there, then either remove the washing off the line or remove the dog from the area when you go out. During puppyhood it is a good idea if you pick up all your pot plants and put them in the front garden where the puppy cannot get to them. When grown up, you can start putting them all back again. For special plants which you cannot remove like you can flower pots, insert four stakes with wire netting around them for protection.

If your dog dashes into the house and jumps over the furniture, put it on the leash when outside, then take it inside. As soon as it tries to jump on to a piece of furniture, say 'No' or 'Off', give the dog a firm and effective jerk on the leash and, as soon as it responds, praise it quietly. You may have to do this a few times as you take it into different rooms. When you think it has got the message and has calmed down, remove the leash and collar. Later, just the word of reproof should be sufficient provided you keep your eye on the dog. Convey to it the impression that you are *always* watching.

You can apply the same sort of correction to stop your dog jumping up at visitors. Naturally the reason why dogs jump up is because they are pleased to see people. However, it is unacceptable and although you still wish your dog to greet people, you have to deter it from jumping up. So, having put it on the leash, take the dog to the front door, open it and invite the visitors inside. If the dog jumps up, say 'No' or 'Off', immediately jerk downwards and, as soon as you see the dog respond by

Fig. 20. If your dog jumps up at a person, say 'No' or 'Off' and, taking hold of the clip part of the leash with the left hand, jerk downwards quickly. Let go and praise the dog quietly as it responds by remaining on the ground.

Fig. 21. Every suitable opportunity should be taken to socialise your puppy with other dogs.

just standing there, quietly praise it. Then ask the visitors if they would be so kind as to step outside the front door again, close the door for a couple of seconds and re-enact the whole entry. A dog will soon learn when you repeat this a few times.

So remember the golden rule — put the dog on the leash first, then you will have the means of control in correcting it if and when necessary and, as you do this, you will uphold your commands and gain the dog's respect. All the corrections are very simple and when applied with common sense, understanding and patience these problems can be overcome (Fig. 20).

There always seems to be so much to teach people when they first come with their dogs for training. While most of them have had dogs before, usually when they were children, for others it is the first dog they have owned.

However, I believe one of the first things people should learn about dogs is how to meet strange dogs (Fig. 21) and how they should introduce their own dogs to other people (Fig. 22).

I find the easiest way of showing this is by example. When they arrive I always remain where I am and ask them to approach me and allow their dog to come straight up to me on the full length of the leash and sniff me all over. As each dog does this, I talk to it slowly and quietly to gain its confidence. Dogs vary in the time they take to become acquainted with people, and when they have I stroke them gently. Having done this, I then shake hands with the owners. Many owners are puzzled at first as to why I get acquainted with their dogs before

Fig. 22. All puppies should be introduced to people in the street.

I actually shake hands with them, so I go on to explain why.

Dogs fall into three main categories. Most dogs are friendly, in fact some are so friendly that they would lick you to death, others are reserved and display varying degrees of suspicion, while a few can be aggressive even to the point that they are positively dangerous.

I then go on to explain that if I approached them instead of asking them to come towards me, I could have a threatening effect on their dogs and this would be most undesirable when the dog first comes for training. Furthermore, if dogs saw me stretch out my hand to shake hands with their owners, suspicious dogs might well retreat, and I most certainly don't want that to happen. And if I shook hands immediately with the owner of a dog with aggressive tendencies, the dog

might think that I was about to hit the owner and consequently bite me.

I also explain to each owner that it is essential for the dog to be on a slack leash. If it is tight and wound around the owner's hand several times to shorten it, the dog will feel so restricted that it is likely to panic if it is suspicious, or lunge forward and bite if it is protectively aggressive. This is because it is so closely and tightly linked to the owner. Another thing that I point out to dog owners is that when I meet a dog for the first time, particularly one which is unsure, I never look into its eyes, but away to one side. If you look a suspicious dog in the eyes you can make it worse. So let it get to know you first in its own time. When you feel that the dog has settled you can look at its eyes without disturbing it.

One of the worst cases of suspicion

17

that I have ever seen happened several years ago, when a fireman and his wife rescued a dog which had been chained up on a short chain in a backyard for several weeks. It had actually been in two homes prior to that, and been ill-treated. When they brought the dog to me it was so frightened that it would not come near me. After repeated attempts I told them not to try bringing the dog up to me any more because she only hid behind them to seek security and was getting herself in a worse state. Instead, I handed them a 170cm (5ft 7in) leather leash which they clipped to her collar and holding the other end of the leash I quietly and slowly led her away from her owners down the driveway and on to the road which was very quiet at that time of the day. Because she had no one to hide behind any longer, it made my task easier in coaxing her towards me. The longer leash gave her a much larger area of independence and walking on the road gave me plenty of open space in which there was nothing which she could get behind to seek refuge. She was so terrified that when I glanced at her eyes I was astonished to see that they had glazed over, just like you would see in an old dog which had gone blind. I could not believe it, I had never seen this sort of thing before. Because she was so frightened, she also passed wind, the smell of which was like chronic diarrhoea, but she did not actually pass any motion as would have been expected when a dog is in that state.

However, being on the long leash she started to settle down and during the next 10 minutes I gradually pulled her in, bit by bit, until she was quite close to me. Then I stroked her gently and talked to her very quietly, and was very careful not to look down into her eyes because this would have possibly frightened her again. As I have said, it is always best to look slightly away from the dog when it is in this state of fear. Although it took time she gradually became used to me and built up a bit of confidence in herself. And so the first lesson was taken up by just gaining the dog's confidence and showing the owners how to walk her on a long leash, getting used to everything in the street, and how to use their voices to encourage her.

When they came the next week, the dog was very much better and seemed to take to me quite well. Then we noticed an even greater improvement on her third visit, for she could not get up the drive quickly enough to see me! She was so happy, and we were all very pleased with her progress.

From then on she put so much trust in her owners and built up a tremendous relationship with me. She just loved coming for training and this was borne out in the way she showed great excitement in their car when they came every week and when they were within half a kilometre (⅓ mile) of my training school. She took to obedience training very well indeed and at the same time we gradually got her used to people. We periodically took her up to a small shopping centre where there were not too many people, and just walked her freely on the leash, allowing her to move about and gradually go up to and sniff people, some of whom we would ask to talk very quietly to her, which they did.

This took months and months to do, and I am happy to say that the couple were well rewarded for their patient efforts. I guess they had rescued that dog just in time. It was a case of pure suspicion, and not nervousness which is considered to be a hereditary fault. It was a great shame that the dog had been in those three terrible homes and chained to a stake in the back garden, but I think you can learn a lot from this story. There was a lovely dog who, in my opinion, had been bred well, but had not been looked after and treated properly in those three homes. That is a story with a happy ending, but there are many more which end in disaster.

Not all cases of dogs becoming suspicious are the result of owners mistreating or handling them incorrectly, or failing to make every effort to introduce them to people. Regrettably, I have seen some very bad heavy handling from judges in the show rings, so much so that I wonder at times how on earth they ever gained their judges' licences. A threatening approach and rough, quick, thoughtless handling from a judge can so easily have an adverse effect on the temperament of a puppy. A puppy only needs to have one unpleasant experience in the show ring and it will then build up in its mind a bad association of ideas, and expect that every judge is going to be like that whenever it is shown in the ring. Is it any wonder then that the animal backs off? Now the question is, can this problem be cured? Yes, in many cases it can, but it usually takes time and a lot depends on how bad the problem is. First of all, I would advise owners whose dogs

Fig. 23. A dog should always be prevented from hiding behind its handler, otherwise this becomes a habit.

have developed this form of fear, to keep their dogs out of shows until the problem has been overcome. If they continue to keep showing them, they are likely to get progressively worse, because they are being subjected to an environment which they do not like.

The next thing to do is to get these dogs used to being handled with care by friends coming into the home and meeting people out on the street so that the dog gradually builds up confidence in you and in itself. With regard to handling a dog of this nature, and in fact any dog, I always advise people never to allow their dogs to get behind them when they are approaching someone (**Fig. 23**). If this is allowed to happen, the dog will keep

Fig. 24. Every effort should be made to introduce the dog to people by putting it out in front and giving it support with reassuring praise.

on doing it to seek security behind the owner. It is very much like a shy child who hides behind his or her mother when she meets someone in the street, whereupon she makes the situation worse by saying that her child is shy. That is about the worst thing she could say. What she needs to do of course is to encourage her child to say 'Hello' to the person. And so when a puppy tries to hide behind you, quickly run your left hand down the leash to prevent this from happening and guide it out in front of you slightly, praise it and encourage it up to people (**Fig. 24**). If you do this consistently, the dog will soon learn that it is not allowed to hide behind you and at the same time you should see an improvement in its confidence. When the dog has overcome these fears, you can then think of returning to showing again even though you may have had to stay away for many weeks. So be patient, take everything carefully, and you will get there in the end!

2 The Second Lesson

When people come to me for their second lesson, I notice that, as they get their dogs out of their cars and walk up my driveway, they generally have much more control than they did the week before. I then ask them how they have been getting on with their dogs during the last week and most will declare that they have been managing reasonably well and now feel more confident in themselves. Up until they came for their first lesson they did not have a clue as to what to do when their dogs misbehaved.

But a lot will admit that, although they felt they had made progress, they could not remember everything. This is quite natural in learning any subject, and so about 10 minutes revision of what was done in the previous lesson soon brings everything back to mind and then we move on to teaching the dog more exercises.

It does not take long at all to show the right-about, right and left turns in heelwork and also how to correct a crooked sit. This is all the average dog owner needs in heelwork. There are many more exercises, such as left-about turn, dropping and standing the dog, walking in the shape of a figure eight around two people, heeling at a very slow pace and also at a fast pace. All these extra exercises only need to be taught if people wish to compete in obedience trials, but only a very small percentage of members in any dog club will have the desire to compete. However, obedience trials can be great fun.

Now to have a close look at the three basic turns. I shall explain the simple and correct way of doing each in order to get quick and good results, and state the common problems which do and can arise if and when the handler falters in some way or another when training his or her dog to do the turns.

Right-about turn

This would be the first turn that I would teach any dog regardless of whether I was training an individual or a class of handlers with their dogs. Up until now you have held the leash in your right hand in the centre of your body when walking your dog at heel in a straight line. You will no-

Fig. 25. *Right-about turn.*
Take hold of all three pieces of leash in one grasp with your left hand and remove your right hand from the two loops it was holding.

Fig. 26. Keeping both hands down at the same level as your dog's neck height is from the ground, pat your right leg rapidly a few times as you say in an interesting tone 'Rex, heel'.

tice that you have three pieces of leash hanging down (**Fig. 25**). Take hold of these three pieces of leash in one grasp with your left hand and remove your right hand from the two loops it was holding. You will now have your right hand perfectly free to pat your right leg at the same height as that of your dog's neck from the ground (**Fig. 26**). The noise made when you slap your leg rapidly a few times as you say, in a very interesting tone, 'Rex, heel!' should attract the dog to come around as you pick your feet up and turn around on the spot. As soon as you see its head respond to come around, praise it vocally (**Fig. 27**). As soon as you have turned around continue walking in a straight line along the line

on which you were walking prior to doing the right-about turn. As you walk all that remains to be done is to put your right hand back through the two loops of leash and you are back to normal again.

This is all right if everything goes nicely! Now for the possible bad news! It might well happen that your dog becomes distracted, say towards another dog, just when you are at the point of doing the turn. If this happens, don't worry, because you have already taken hold of the leash in your left hand in one grasp (whereby there should exist about 30cm (1ft) of leash between your left hand and the clip of your leash) and if you keep your left hand down on your left knee

Fig. 27. As the dog responds in turning, praise it vocally.

Fig. 28. If the dog does not respond, give a quick, short, horizontal jerk and relax the leash immediately.

(providing that the height from the ground is the same as the dog's neck height from the ground), you are then in the ideal position to give the dog a quick, short, sharp, horizontal jerk in the direction you wish to go if it does not instantly obey your command. If, and only if, you have to give such jerks to uphold your command, always ensure that your left hand returns instantly to your left knee so that the 30cm (1ft) of leash hangs in a U shape once again (**Fig. 28**).

If you have a medium-size dog like a Labrador or a German Shepherd, you would need to hold your left hand down to about your knee height. If you are training a large dog like a fully grown Great Dane then you won't need to bend down at all, but if you are training something small like a Welsh Corgi or Dachshund then you need to put your hands down to about ankle height! It can be a bit back-breaking I know, but the point to remember is always to get down to the respective height of the dog you are training.

You will find that the right-about turn is very easy to do provided you carry out this procedure. However, things can and do go wrong because of incorrect handling. The most common faults are dogs walking wide, pulling outwards on the leash, being inattentive, going slow, being scent distracted or even jumping all over their handlers and mouthing their hands.

The causes of all these problems are clearly seen. Firstly, a lot of handlers don't prepare their leash and get their hands in the proper positions and start talking to the dog while they are walking along just prior to executing the turn. Instead, they turn first, then possibly say heel afterwards and pull the leash tight and up in the air. Their dogs are not even given a chance of knowing what is required.

Secondly, many handlers don't turn around on the spot, but do large U turns whereby the dogs drift wide for fear of being stepped onto. On the other hand, some handlers do very good footwork but sometimes stop in the middle of a turn. This breaks the continuity. The dogs then stop and wonder what they have to do next.

Thirdly, there are a great number of handlers who do not praise their dogs immediately they respond, or if they do they don't say the words of praise sincerely and enthusiastically enough in order to give their dogs an incentive and reward for a turn well done.

Fourthly, some dogs are given far too many right-about turns until they get fed up to the teeth with the whole business and their willingness to work drops considerably. I have seen this happen on numerous occasions at dog training clubs where classes have been continuously marched up and down the field. My advice to instructors in this regard is for them to demonstrate really well to show handlers how to do the turns, after which the handlers should do only a few in the practical sessions.

Lastly, even though handlers have been shown how to prepare, how to keep their dogs' attention, how to talk to the dog, how to hold the leash and how to carry out their footwork, they still tend to make one very common mistake. They may pull the leash tight as their dogs come around, which causes them to pull outwards. Let me explain how this effect takes place. Imagine you have tied a weight onto one end of a piece of string about a metre (1yd) long, and then set it in motion by whirling it around above your head a few times. The effect is that the weight pulls outwards because of its centrifugal force, consequently when you let go of the string, the weight hurls through the air and possibly straight through someone's window! Well, the effect is very similar when doing a right-about turn on a tight leash, only this time the weight on the end is the dog. So when carrying out a right-about turn, keep your eyes on the leash as well as the dog; keep that 30cm (1ft) of leash slack in a U shape and, if you have to give the required jerk, slacken the leash instantly.

Right turn

Having taught your dog the right-about turn, you will find it very easy to do the right turn. It is carried out in the same way as the right-about turn except of course you will only have to turn at 90° to the right instead of 180°. But, with regard to footwork, there is one point I feel needs mentioning. In order to get the best attention from your dog when you turn right, turn sharply to the right with both feet together on the spot and then proceed in the new direction (**Fig. 29a**). Your dog, upon hearing your command, 'Rex, heel!', and the noise of your right hand slapping your right

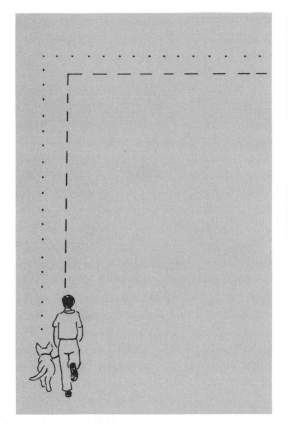

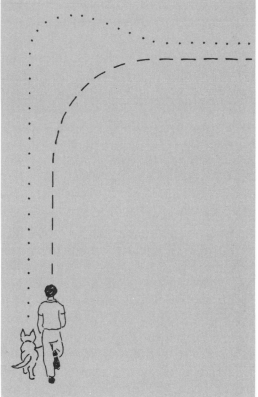

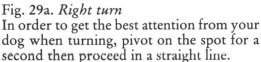

Fig. 29a. *Right turn*
In order to get the best attention from your dog when turning, pivot on the spot for a second then proceed in a straight line.

Fig. 29b. If you turn gradually to the right in a quarter of a circle, the turn is not defined clearly enough and the dog is likely to walk straight on and perform a wide turn on a tight leash.

leg, will suddenly see you change direction and go with you. When it responds, praise it immediately. If you carry out a right turn by gradually going around in a quarter of a circle, commonly called a right wheel, you will lose the effect of capturing the best attention from your dog (**Fig. 29b**). Attention from your dog is what you need, not only in preliminary training but in continuing stages right up to and including advanced work, if you ever want to go that far. So, regardless of the purpose for which

I am going to train a dog, I always do sharp right turns in order to get 'the best attention I can from the dog. Any faults which happen in the right turn are the same as I have mentioned with the right-about turn and of course the same advice applies.

Left turn

I always think that this turn is the easiest of them all. With this turn you don't have to transfer the leash from one hand to the other as explained

25

when doing right-about and right turns.

Carry the leash in your right hand as you normally do while heeling your dog and, when you have decided to turn left, just take hold of the leash near the clip with your left hand (with your thumb on the top), give a quick command, 'Heel', and jerk the leash straight back horizontally along the dog's back. This should stop the dog abruptly, but only for a fraction of a second. Now in that fraction of a second, spin on the ball of your left foot towards the left and bring your right foot around and continue walking in the new direction. You should let go of the leash immediately you have given the backward jerk with your left hand. The purpose of the jerk is to stop the dog advancing any further forward, and should be given just as your left foot is about to come down on the ground. Make sure that you do not stop, but keep on the move as you step around with your right foot, which is the outside foot as far as your dog is concerned. Later, when the dog sees your body turn and your right foot come around, it will turn its head in the same direction and its body will follow.

The main problem seen with the left turn is where the handler has to literally battle to get around in front of the dog. Apart from it being a huge struggle, the handler often treads on the dog's paws or knees the dog in the side of the face. It is not unusual to see a handler go head-over-heels over the dog, which can be most upsetting for the dog and frustrating for the handler.

Once again, such faults are either caused by the handler not carrying out the correct procedure for the left turn, or he or she may have been instructed incorrectly in the first place.

Firstly, the fault is usually caused by the handler not jerking back firmly enough and at the right angle. Often the dog is jerked upwards, which does not stop the dog going any further forward. Sometimes the handler tries to jerk the dog to the left, which only pushes the dog away and doesn't stop it.

Secondly, the fault is caused by bad footwork. Often the handler steps across in front of the dog with his or her left foot. This eventually causes the dog to be afraid of the handler's foot and it then walks wide. Some handlers turn and then stop for a second or two. In that very short time their dogs seize the opportunity of stepping straight forward again instead of turning to the left.

Thirdly, the command, 'Heel', is not always used firmly and said quickly enough. It should be said in such a way as to convey to the dog, 'Get back while I get around!'; very much like you say if you need to correct your dog when it goes too far ahead while you are heeling in a straight line.

I never use the dog's name when doing left turns as I do with the other two turns in the early days of training. There is a reason for this. When training a dog to do a right-about or a right turn, the dog is on the outside — you are therefore actually calling the dog around you. And so it is advantageous to use the dog's name. But, with the left turn, the dog is not being called around, it is being told to stop or to hold back while you step around it. That is the difference. Eventually no commands or physical actions are needed. The dog, having been taught the right way, will instantly recognise by the way in which you turn what it is required to do. But like everything else, the dog must be taught properly in the first place.

At this stage of the training I believe it is of great benefit for handlers to learn how to correct any crooked sits their dogs will have from time to time. Up until this time I advise handlers to just pull their dogs into their left sides and make them sit. This is alright for the first week as they have so many other things to concentrate on. But now I tell them that if they continued to rely on that procedure, their dogs would continue to let them do it, and the handlers would be doing all the work! Thus the dog has to be taught to get up on all fours and come in close to the handler's left side and sit straight. This corrective exercise is commonly known as the correction of the crooked sit. It is not hard to do, in fact it is very easy to apply if you follow the diagrams and study the photographs (Fig. 30).

Suppose your dog is sitting in a crooked position, and is also too far ahead of you. Place your left hand on the leash near the clip with your thumb on the top, and ensure that your left hand is at the same height from the ground as the dog's neck height is from the ground (Fig. 31). Keeping your right foot where it is and facing in the direction you have been going, cast your left foot back one good stride and in a slight arc behind your right foot, and bend at your knees as you

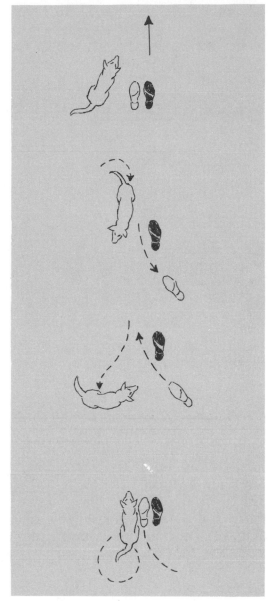

Fig. 30. (a) The dog is sitting in a crooked position.
(b) The handler's right foot remains still, while he or she takes the left foot back in an arc, simultaneously leading the dog with the left hand as indicated.
(c) As it turns towards the handler's left foot, the left foot is taken forward to the right foot.
(d) The dog follows and is made to sit straight and close beside the handler.

Fig. 31. The dog is sitting crooked and slightly too far forward.

Fig. 32. Stepping back with the left foot, the command is given, 'Prince, heel!', and the dog follows the left hand.

do so. As you do this, command the dog in a very inviting tone, 'Prince, heel!', enticing it to follow your left hand (which holds the leash near the clip) and turn in towards you (**Fig. 32**), then slightly away as it comes back, and then in towards you again (**Fig. 33**). As it does the last turn, bring your left foot forward to your right foot. The dog, thinking you are going forward, will come in beside you, whereupon you make it sit (**Fig. 34**). Make quite sure that, as it comes forward and in close to your side, you have both your hands ready in the correct position in order to make it sit straight. Just like other aspects of heelwork, ensure that your left hand holds the leash at the dog's height until you make it sit. That part of the leash must then be quickly transferred to

the right hand and held up vertically above the dog's head as you push downwards and forwards with your left hand on the dog's hindquarters. During this correction, praise the dog as it responds, so that it associates the correction with pleasure.

This corrective exercise is invaluable because it can be used in so many different ways. For example, it can be used with crooked stands and drops. Naturally the appropriate command 'Stand' or 'Drop' has to be given as the dog comes into your side, otherwise it might automatically sit. It can also be used if the dog goes far too far forward in heelwork or even when the dog is walking freely on a long leash and you want to bring it into heel.

The next major exercise to teach the

Fig. 33. As the dog comes back, it is guided in towards the left foot.

Fig. 34. The dog follows the left foot which is brought forward, whereupon the dog is made to sit straight.

dog is to stay in the sitting position. I always find it rather amusing when I have said, 'We will now teach the dog to "Stay"!' Most owners give a grin of utter defeat and say, 'Well, that is something I know it will not do! I've tried and tried, but it just keeps getting up!' Upon asking them further questions I frequently learn that they have been expecting the dog to stay in one room while they go out of sight into another, without teaching the dog the preliminaries. There are a number of reasons why a dog will not stay and most of them are caused in the early days of training.

When you teach any dog to sit and stay, the very first thing that you must do is to make a mental note of where you have actually told the dog to sit and stay and the direction in which

you have faced it. If it moves from there you must take it back to the very same spot and start all over again. If it moves forward a metre (1yd) or so and you tell it to stay again, then you have allowed it to move to another place, and it will have won! That is the beginning of having a creeping dog, and the fault will soon develop into a major problem in which the dog will not stay at all.

When you command it to 'Stay', say this *without* the dog's name. If you use its name, it is quite likely to walk off with you because you have used its name in heelwork. When you leave the dog to take up your position in front to face it, do not walk straight out because if it sees your feet proceed in that direction, it will naturally think that that is heelwork and follow you.

Fig. 35. When leaving your dog in the early days of a sit-stay exercise, step around with the right foot towards the dog.

Instead, turn your feet around to face the dog as you adopt that position out in front of it (Fig. 35). Always be ready to check it if it moves by holding the leash in your left hand about half a metre (18in) vertically above its head, so that you can immediately say 'Sit' and give an upward jerk on the leash. But be sure to relax the leash immediately. In order to carry out this first stage of the exercise you need to be standing one straight arm's length away. This is a very good example of

yet another principle of training, namely, always be in a position to do something if the dog makes a wrong move. Accept the fact that your dog will probably move. It is not a case of it being disobedient, but a simple case of it not really knowing at this stage what you want it to do. It is a new exercise, so be patient.

If your dog gets up and completely moves away from the spot on which you told it to 'Stay', the quickest and simplest way to correct the fault is to immediately return to your original place, facing in the original direction in which you gave the command 'Stay', and bring the dog to heel by using the crooked sit correction. Command it to 'Sit', then to 'Stay', and start all over again.

Don't leave the dog for too long, especially if it is young, because its concentration will not last for very long. Return to it by the same way that you left its side. If you return by walking around the back of it, the dog is likely to get up and turn around to see what you are doing. When you do arrive back at its side, don't praise it immediately you get there, because in future lessons when it sees you even start to return, it is likely to anticipate your praise and may get up and come to meet you. Instead, each time you return stand at its side for a varying number of seconds and then praise it. This will keep it guessing as to when you have decided that the exercise is over.

I am sure that you can now understand how mistakes can cause a dog to falter and if you don't take these necessary precautions you will surely have problems. If anything does go wrong, I would always advise that you go back to the beginning again, and that applies to any exercise. It is in fact another recognised principle in training. So remember, keep your eyes constantly on your dog and correct it the instant it moves.

This brings me to another problem, which is that people's reflexes are too slow in correcting their dogs. If a dog knows that it can get away with something for even a second or two, it will. So how can people quicken their reflexes? For years I have seen many instructors attempt to get people to act quickly. Instructors who are excellent demonstrators are able to get some handlers to copy them and get good results, but other handlers are still slow. I have seen instructors endeavour to get the handlers in a class to sit their dogs quickly by counting from one upwards, hoping that it would make them work quickly. But this was of little use, or none at all. Some sat their dogs by the time the instructor said three, a few more by four and five and the rest by six and so on.

Then several years ago I devised a training method to make people quicker. Strange how things happen, but it was actually the result of my attendance at evening classes where I was studying the motion of falling bodies in physics. While holding some small object, like a pencil or bunch of keys, about 1.3m (4ft) above the ground, I would ask the handler or even a large audience of people in a dog training club to watch carefully and say the word 'No!' very quickly between the time I let go of the object and before it reached the ground.

Knowing what they had to do, I would go on talking about something else in order to try to distract them. With eyes concentrating 100 per cent and having the word on the tips of their tongues, a spontaneous 'No!' was suddenly projected towards me as I released the object from my hand. I would always congratulate them, and then do it once more, but the second time I would hold the object about 75cm (30in) above the ground or a table so that they could all see. They would realise that they had a very limited time to say 'No!', but nevertheless it was a challenge. Once again their quick response was tremendous and furthermore it was seen that they all seemed to enjoy it and had a good laugh about it.

So over the years I have continued to use this method and have found it extremely effective, because it does three things; it makes them concentrate, it quickens their reflexes and they learn to ignore all distractions. When they all do this so well, I tell them that is how they should watch their dogs, how quick they must be in giving corrections and how they must ignore all distractions surrounding them when training their dogs.

When the first stage of the sit-stay has been taught, I advise people to use it in practical ways every day. For instance, when you are going out, sit the dog near the front door, tell it to 'Stay', open the door, heel the dog outside on the leash, tell it to 'Sit' and 'Stay' again as you shut the door, then heel towards your car. Sit the dog. Tell it to 'Stay' as you open the car door. Wait a few seconds, tell the dog to get in, praise it on response and shut the door. If it anticipates and tries to get in before you tell it, say 'No!', and jerk it back. Shut the door and go through the procedure again. You can apply the same procedure when getting a dog out of a car. It does not take long.

So always remember, if you are prepared to devote a little bit of time, thought, effort and consistent training, you will be greatly rewarded with the love and respect your dog has for you. Without that respect many problems are bound to emerge.

3　The Recall

When people telephone me to make an appointment for training, I always ask them if they have any problems with their dogs. Quite a few people say that they don't really have any problems, in fact they are very pleased with the way their dogs have settled into their homes, but would like to do the right thing by learning how to train them properly. I always like to hear dog owners say something like this, because it shows that they have an excellent attitude to owning dogs. Most people however are very quick to tell me that they have problems with their dogs, and like the other people, they also wish to do the right thing by learning how to train their pets properly. At the same time they are naturally anxious to know whether or not it is possible to overcome the problems they have with their dogs.

One of the most common problems people have is that their dogs won't come when they are called. This can be disastrous if a dog gets out on to the road or gets loose and starts to worry livestock. I know how frustrating it can be when a dog won't come when called, but how can it be

expected to come if it does not respect its owner and if it has not been taught the exercise properly. There are a few cases where dogs do come when called even though they have not received any formal training, but when you take a close look at these cases you generally find that they are dogs which lack initiative and are quite content to hang around their owners, mainly for security.

I like to teach dogs to come when their owners attend their third training lesson and, as with all other training exercises, I start by teaching the dog to come on the leash. It is known as the recall exercise, because you are recalling your dog.

Having taught the dog very basic heelwork, which includes the forward, the sit, the three turns and the sit-stay exercise, you will have earned a lot of respect from your dog. That is a great start, because you have laid a good foundation on which to build. Next is the recall, which is not as hard to teach as many people think it will be. In fact, it is really quite simple.

With your dog on the leash sitting beside you, tell it to stay, turn around to face it, step back about a metre (1yd), and at the same time extend your hand which is holding only the handle of the leash. Wait a few seconds, then say 'Sam, come!' and bend down. Your action will stimulate the dog to respond and as soon as you see it take the *first* step towards you, praise it, 'Good dog', and walk backwards slowly. Take up half the length of the leash in one hand so that the dog does not get its legs tangled in it and keep both your hands situated in between your knees, which should entice it to you. Concentrate on walking backwards slowly in a perfectly straight line. If the dog does divert to your left or right, maintain your straight course and, with your spare hand, take hold of the clip part of the leash, say 'Come', and give the dog a horizontal jerk to bring it straight in front of you again. Praise it immediately and let go of the clip part of the leash. Repeat this correction whenever necessary. The dog will soon realise that if it goes to the left or right of you it will be corrected, but if it comes directly and straight to you it will be praised.

As soon as you have gained reasonably good results for a few metres (yards), gather in the rest of the leash in one hand and, with your other hand over the dog's hindquarters, say 'Sit'. As you stop, pull the leash up vertically above the dog's head into your chest and at the same time push its hindquarters down and towards you with your other hand. Immediately praise the dog by allowing it to rest its chin in the fingers of both your hands and stroke it slowly with your thumbs from its eyes back towards its ears. Prolong this praise and do not

allow the dog to look around. If it does, say 'No, leave!' and give it one quick shake with both hands, then say 'Good dog' as it looks at you. After you have praised it for several seconds, stand beside it, walk it at heel for a few metres, then do another recall. One of the best places to do recalls is on a quiet, straight, narrow footpath, as it helps you to keep straight and this is important. You need to make it as simple as possible for your dog to understand.

I always believe in giving a dog prolonged vocal and physical praise, because in the immediate future when you want to give your dog a free run in some park, for instance, just think of all the distractions it is going to have, namely other dogs, children playing and thousands of smells. And all you have as a reward is your praise. So when you teach your dog to come, give it an incentive by really piling on the praise.

I well remember one lady who was always cuddling and kissing her dog when it did well. Although one could readily understand how pleased she was at the time, the dog would then act silly and the training was spoilt. One day she arrived at my place in plenty of time and while I was finishing writing a letter in my front room I heard her get the dog out of her car and give it a little training up and down the footpath. I could not see them because of the high thick hedge in my front garden. However, after about 5 minutes, I went out. Following greeting her, I said, 'I heard you giving your dog a little bit of training. Is everything going all right?'. 'Oh, yes,' she replied. 'I am so very pleased

Fig. 36. When the dog is walking quite freely on the leash and out in front, call it, 'Sam, come!', praise it the instant it responds and walk slowly backwards.

Fig. 37. As the dog comes to you, take up half the length of the leash so that it does not get its legs tangled. Keep both hands situated between your knees to entice the dog to you.

with him. He is heeling nicely, sitting and staying on command and is coming quite well on the leash'. As I looked down at her yellow Labrador, and he looked up at me in glee, I could not resist making the remark, 'Yes, and when I heard you call him you kissed him when he came and sat at your feet!' 'Well, yes, I must confess I did', she admitted, 'but how do you know? You couldn't see through that thick high hedge'. 'That's true! I can't', I added, 'but you've left a beautiful lipstick mark on top of his head!'

This basic recall should also be done when you are walking your dog free on the leash. When it is walking out in front of you, seize the opportunity of recalling it by giving the command, 'Sam, come!', and as soon as it responds by turning around to come to you, praise it and walk backwards (**Fig. 36**). The rest of the recall should be carried out as previously explained (**Figs 37, 38** and **39**). If the dog does

not respond within 1 second of your initial command, bend down and give it one horizontal jerk on the leash towards you to uphold your command, then give praise immediately it responds even though you have made it do so.

The next stage in the recall from the sit-stay position should be done in a safe, enclosed area where you can discreetly drop the leash from your hand as you tell the dog to 'Stay' and leave it. As you step around to face it and walk backwards a few paces, have your left arm outstretched with fist clenched as if you still have hold of the leash (**Fig. 40**). This is a crafty way of doing it, as the dog, seeing you adopt that position, thinks that you still have it on the leash! As you call it, your hand movements, with the imaginary leash, should be the same as when you taught it to come on the real leash (**Fig. 41**). The dog will recognise these movements which you have been doing

35

Fig. 38. As you walk back and the dog comes in, prepare it to sit by taking up all the leash in one hand and placing the other hand over the hindquarters. Say 'Sit!' Hold the leash above the dog's head as you push the hindquarters down and towards you.

Fig. 39. Immediately praise your dog by allowing it to rest its chin in the fingers of both your hands. Stroke it slowly with your thumbs from the eyes to the ears.

consistently for the last few days. As it gets to you, take hold of the clip part of the leash and sit the dog (**Fig. 42**).

Doing the recall, with your dog dragging the leash along the ground, is only necessary for, say, 2 or 3 days. It is an interim period between doing the recall on the leash and totally off the leash. It has great advantages. If, for instance, the dog just sits and refuses to come after you have called a couple of times, then you can step forward, pick up the leash, give a jerk towards you and, as soon as it responds, praise it and let go of the leash again. On the other hand, it may come immediately and try to run past you. If this happens, quickly put your foot on the leash, pick it up and apply the necessary correction.

The next stage is to do all this in the presence of another dog, which acts as a distraction, once again in an enclosed, safe area. At this stage of training, I take my clients into my back garden which measures approximately 15m by 18m (50ft by 60ft). I then get my assistant, a fully grown German Shepherd dog, to lie down, and ask my client to carry out the recall with his or her dog on the leash so that it has to come right past my dog. If the dog does show signs of distraction towards mine, which is to be expected, the owner gives the necessary corrections and insists that it comes. Once again, you can readily see here that the owner is gaining respect from his or her dog. The next stage is for the owner to drop the leash, position himself or herself a few

Fig. 40. Having told your dog to 'Stay', stand a few paces away with your left arm outstretched with fist clenched as if you still have hold of the leash.

Fig. 41. The dog recognises the hand movements and comes in straight.

Fig. 42. As it reaches you, take hold of the clip part of the leash and sit the dog.

metres past my German Shepherd dog and call the dog (**Figs 43 and 44**). In most cases the dog comes straight away, but if there is the slightest indication of diversion towards mine, the owner must quickly say 'No! Come!' and 'Good dog!' the moment it responds. If these words are not obeyed, the owner must then step forward and correct the dog with the necessary correction on the leash. It is all very simple if taken through the gradual stages.

The next stage is when the two dogs meet and play with each other. While they are playing, I ask my client to call his or her dog. If the dog does not come, then it is put on the leash and the exercise is repeated, until it does come. Finally when it does come, it receives prolonged sincere praise, and the exercise finishes on that good note.

Fig. 43. The dog being trained to come in the presence of another dog.

Fig. 44. Even when the dog is being praised it should not be allowed to look around until told to 'Go free'.

In fact, I now have a little notice on the inside of my gate which says 'No dog leaves this enclosure until it has done a recall!'

Occasionally, I do get a very strong, self-willed dog which will not obey, but I always adopt the attitude, and I tell my clients to do the same, that I am going to win! It does not matter how long it takes. If your dog has x amount of willpower, make sure that your willpower is $x+1$. It will give in eventually and, no matter how naughty it has been, praise the dog as soon as it has responded. I know a lot of patience is required at times and a lot of self-discipline on your part in being firm and not losing your temper, but believe me you will feel great when you have accomplished a recall and your dog will feel good on receiving your prolonged, loving praise.

I generally advise people to train their dogs for about 15 to 20 minutes a day, sometimes longer if and when they get up to the higher realms of obedience where there are so many more exercises to perform. But no matter what stage of training you are at, it is a good idea to allow the dog to relax in between certain exercises. There are of course exceptions to the rule and these are often seen when you have to deal with a dog which has strong willpower and high initiative.

Years ago a lady brought a black Labrador to me for basic training. He was very clever and very naughty! He soon learnt how to heel, sit, stay and come on the leash, but when given a free run in the park, he would run off and it would take over half an hour to catch him. Things were becoming worse instead of better.

38

One particular afternoon we let him off for a free run in a safe park and, after several attempts to recall him, the only way to catch him was to go to his owner's car and open the door. He then ran and jumped inside, expecting to go home and not have to do any more training! Little did he know that I was not going to tolerate his disobedience and that I was going to put him through his paces again.

So I put him on the leash and had to literally drag him out of the car, to which he stubbornly resisted. Then all of a sudden the heavens opened and we had a torrential thunderstorm. This did not deter me. As there was little point in both of us getting wet, I asked the lady if she would like to sit in her car and watch while I trained her dog. Within a few minutes I was soaked to the skin. That did not worry me at all. It was not a cold day and I knew that I could have a hot shower at home afterwards.

Well, I do not think I have ever come across a Labrador before which was so wilful. I went on and on training him, telling myself that no matter how long it would take, I was going to win. Believe it or not, I trained him for 1 hour and 20 minutes, the last 10 minutes of which was most successful. I had him heeling off the leash, doing fast straight and immediate recalls from the sit position as well as during his free running. Although I had to put a lot of hard work into it at the time, I was highly delighted with the results. Not only did he come instantly, fast and straight, he wagged his tail rapidly with great pleasure and put his nose straight in between my knees as he came in and sat in front of me, after which I praised him abundantly.

The following week I quite expected that we were going to have the same sort of trouble again, but I am happy to say that we did not; in fact, from that time on we never had any more trouble. He could be let off at any time for a free run, even to meet and play with other dogs, and when recalled would always come with great willingness. You could say that we had reached a crisis point in that 80-minute training session and what had been heading for disaster had turned into success.

4 Problems with the Recall

It must always be remembered that the recall is the most important exercise in dog training. It does not matter for what purpose you are training a dog, it must come when called. Without a good recall, you cannot progress any further with more advanced exercises and you will never be able to trust your dog off the leash when you want it to have a free run. A free run every day for every dog is essential for its well-being.

Many people have problems with the recall, and while most of these are caused through the lack of respect the dog has for the owner, a number are caused in other ways.

Perhaps the most common of these is found where owners have played a lot with their dogs. When I say played, I mean they have really had a riotous time in encouraging them to jump up, have rolled them over on the ground, played chasey around the table or things outside and got their dogs highly excited. Is it any wonder then that such dogs lead their owners a merry dance when they want them to come? The dogs interpret the training exercise as continuous playtime

and therefore want to have their own way.

I have often found it amusing when, for instance, I am giving a talk on dog training to a large audience, and a question is asked, 'My dog won't come. He just runs in circles around me, occasionally mouths my hand as he dashes by and it does not matter how much I call him, he just won't come and I can't catch him!' In reply I then ask, 'Madam, have you, since you had your dog as a puppy, played with him? If so, how have you played with him?'. She replies, quite truthfully, that she has played with him very much like she has played with her children when they were young, namely that they have had a good romp and chase around! I then suggest that that is the cause of the problem she is now having. I follow this up immediately by saying that personally I do not play with my dogs! As I say this, my eyes quickly scan the audience, and I notice some very surprised looks on a number of faces. I can imagine some of them saying to themselves, 'This Michael Tucker, he gives us a most interesting talk and now says that he does not play with his dogs! What a heartless fellow!'

I go on to explain why I do not play with my dogs in a riotous and excitable manner. How you play with children is one thing, but if you play in the same way with a dog, which it will enjoy, it is highly likely to react in the same way when you want it to come. Instead, when I let my dog off for a free run in a park, she runs around, picks up sticks, chases after the moths and butterflies and during this whole time I communicate with her by voice, saying something like, 'Go on, off you go! Have you got a stick? Where's the butterfly then? There it goes'. My dog thoroughly enjoys me talking to her and sharing her enjoyment of being able to run free and we enjoy our company together. This is how I like to see a good human-dog relationship. But I would never do anything so foolish as bowling my dog over, trying to grab it, letting it mouth my hands or chasing it around a tree. When I say all this I quickly look at those same faces in the audience and see a complete change. Their expressions reveal that they now understand, for the first time, that what they have done with their dogs in the past has been wrong and they have caused the problem. I then point to and ask some of those people in the audience, 'Have you got that problem, Sir? And you, Madam? And I'm sure the two young ladies sitting over there have it too'. Yes, they are all ready to admit it and we all have a laugh about it. 'OK', I say, 'I guess most of us are guilty of it, or similar things. We do these things with good intentions, but do not realise at the time that we are at fault.

We then go on to blame the poor old dog. Well, we all learn by our mistakes. What we have got to do now is to put it right'.

Another very common problem with the recall is where the dog does a lovely recall, fast, straight, and possibly over a long distance, only to suddenly dash to one side or the other of the handler when it gets within 2 to 3 metres (yards) of him or her. In nearly every case this swerving away has been caused by the handler suddenly stretching out to grab the dog as it gets near. After this has happened a few times, the dog naturally thinks, as it runs towards the handler, no matter from what distance, that the handler is going to pounce on it to grab it. Thus the dog avoids the handler at that point. Can you blame it? Wouldn't you do that if you were the dog? Added to this the handler often turns around again and again, calling the dog in frustration, whereupon the dog literally runs rings around him or her and enjoys the game immensely!

The simple answer to this problem is: never grab your dog! Keep your hands together in between your knees and entice it quietly to your hands. It is important to keep your eyes on your dog and also to keep your feet facing in the original direction from which the dog came initially. Do not turn around, as this is virtually giving in to the dog. It has to learn that 'Come' means that it must come to the front of your body and sit. If it does happen to stop half a metre (18 in) short, just slowly put out your hand, take hold of the collar and gently guide it in to sit in front of you and praise it. The dog will then associate that these are loving hands and not grabbing ones.

I will always remember the late Mr Sandon Moss, an old friend of mine and an excellent trainer in England, saying on a number of occasions, 'The people I find the hardest to train are the voiceless ones and the grabbers!' I could not agree with him more, but it is our job as instructors to teach people how to use their voices and how to use their hands effectively, without over-handling. And sometimes when I am training a person who, out of force of habit, keeps grabbing at the dog as it comes in on a recall, I feel like putting a pair of handcuffs on him or her!

Quite a number of handlers, while they have not been guilty of grabbing at their dogs, have the problem of their dogs overshooting them on the recall exercise. One effective way of curing this fault is to stand with your back to a wall or fence. This will soon make any dog put the brakes on and give you a better chance of getting it to sit in front of you as it comes in. However, you might not always have a wall or fence to help you. Instead you might be right out in the open. So in a case like that, if the dog comes at a fast speed and suddenly goes past you, immediately say 'No' and 'Come' and walk straight forward, turning only your head to keep your eyes on it. As the dog turns to come after you, praise it. 'Good dog', and the moment its nose passes you step backwards saying 'Come' again. As the dog turns to come to the front of you, praise it and sit it in approximately the same place where you had been standing when you first called it. The impor-

tant thing is to keep your feet facing in the same direction, your eyes on the dog all the time during the exercise and get your timing right with the appropriate words of command and praise (**Fig. 45**).

Yet another problem with the recall is one where, although the dog does the recall when and where there are no distractions, it will not come when called if other dogs are in the vicinity. The causes of this are once again created by the owner, in that the dog has not been sufficiently socialised with other dogs on the leash, and that the owner has not been game enough to let the dog off the leash to play with other dogs and then call it back.

If you socialise your dog really well with dogs of all shapes and sizes, it will grow up to accept them so much that eventually you can walk it down the street on the leash, and it will not as much as glance at them. If you do not socialise your dog with others, it will most likely grow up to fear them, be very strongly distracted towards them, or even aggressive towards them.

Quite often I have clients who fear the worst about letting their dogs off the leash when there are other dogs around in the park. I tell them that it is no good evading the issue. You have got to start some time, and now is a good time! After all, you have taught your dog to come and now it is entering a stage when it has to come under all circumstances. You have a job to do, so get on with it.

Very often, when a dog is let off the leash and races over to another dog, it will stop half-way, look at the other dog for a moment, then come

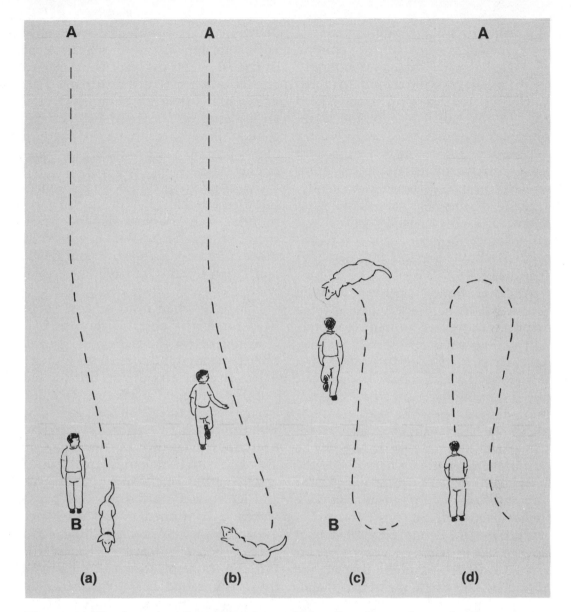

Fig. 45. (a) The dog comes from point A past the handler who stands at point B.
(b) The handler walks forward towards point A, calling the dog which turns and follows.
(c) The dog just passes the handler who then walks backwards towards point B.
(d) The dog comes in straight to sit in front of the handler who is still facing point A.

dashing back to its owner, even though it has not been called. This surprises many owners. Others will race over and meet other dogs and then come racing back, especially when they see their owners walk or run in the opposite direction.

A great number of dogs will not obey the command 'Come' when they are scent distracted. Take the example of a dog which is sniffing at a tree. If it does not show any signs of coming when called a few times, say no more until you have walked straight up to it, clipped the leash on it and stood back at the full length of the leash. Then command 'Come' and give it a horizontal jerk towards you as you walk backwards to the place from which you called the dog originally, praising it as it responds. Having sat it and praised it vocally and physically, let the dog go again and repeat this corrective method if it disobeys again **(Fig. 46)**.

Another similar problem is often seen with male dogs which, having disobeyed several commands to come, will decide to come only after they have, say, lifted a leg to urinate on a tree. Frankly this is bad, because the dog is coming in his own time and not immediately upon the owner's command. It clearly shows a lack of respect and the dog is trying to be dominant over his owner. If the dog is free running, it is quite all right for him to lift his leg on a tree, but once he has been called he must come.

This fault is quite easy to cure if you go about it as soon as you see it start to develop. Put the dog on the leash, let him walk quite freely and, provided he has been given a chance to relieve himself, let him sniff at some more trees. Then suddenly give him the command 'Come'. Give him only 1 second in which to respond and if he does not do so, give him the appropriate jerk towards you and walk backwards. On no account allow him to lift his leg. He will soon learn that he must obey instantly and not pursue his malish instincts when you call him.

Naturally this problem occurs only with male dogs and not bitches, except of course when they are coming into season or are actually in season. This is when the instinct to mate is very strong and the owner of even a well-trained bitch may have to exercise more control over her during that particular time.

As dogs go through their puppyhood, they change. During the early months, they are very dependent on their owners. Then later they become more outgoing, gain more confidence and finally want to have their own way.

One day when my German Shepherd bitch was about 5 months old, I let her off in the park and she ran after two dogs and played with them. I then decided to call her, but she did not obey. I called a few times but my voice seemed to fall on deaf ears! She was about 80m (87 yd) away. I hurried up to her, took her by the scruff of the neck with both hands, said 'Come' and gave her one shake towards me and let go as I started walking backwards. I continued to use my voice every few metres, saying 'Come; good girl!' When I had walked backwards the 80m to the place from which I had originally called her, I made her sit and gave her prolonged praise. I then released her and allowed her to go and play with the two dogs again. After a while, I called her and she came immediately and from that time on she has always come no matter whether she is actually playing with other dogs or running after them.

This brings me to tell you of another problem with recall. Some dog owners let their dogs off for a good

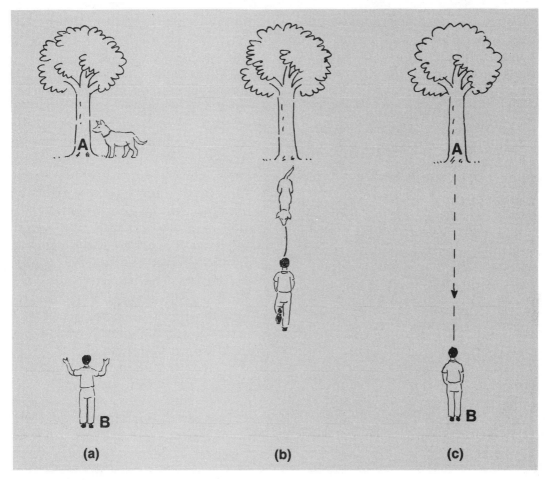

Fig. 46. (a) The dog is scent distracted towards a tree at point A and refuses to come.
(b) The handler proceeds to the dog, clips the leash on and makes the dog come as he walks backwards.
(c) The handler walks backwards to point B from where he had originally called the dog.

free run, call them, put them on leashes and take them home. After a while when these dogs are called they associate it with going home. It may well be that they do not want to go home and they need a greater time to run free. And this is where the dog rebels and refuses to come. So you can see, the cause is the owner once again, who is only giving one free run, one recall and taking the dog home. The owner needs to do several free runs and recalls, so that when the dog comes it can expect to be dismissed again for another free run and so on until the owner considers it has had an adequate amount of exercise and the dog will be quite happy to go home. Makes you think, doesn't it? And that is the whole point. You have to try and put yourselves in the dog's position, and try and see things from its point of view and try to understand how its mind really ticks.

45

A few years ago I was training a lady with her dog who was in its final stages of training and they were both doing extremely well. I asked her to let it off for a free run in the park, which she did and it ran off about 50m (55yd) away and played with a Dobermann Pinscher whose owner was walking about the same distance away in the opposite direction. Incidentally, he had been taking his dog to an obedience dog club. I then asked my client to call her dog, which she did and it came immediately. So too did this Dobermann and it stood beside her as she was praising her dog. In the meantime, the owner of the Dobermann was frantically calling his dog, and after several calls his dog raced back to him. Whereupon he took hold of his dog and started beating him with the leash. I immediately called out to him to stop it and strode over to him. I was very angry and said, 'Don't you ever let me see you hit your dog again! You ought to be ashamed of yourself. Your young dog has a lovely temperament and obviously wants to please. What you need to do,' I said, 'is to praise your dog when he comes, not punish him. As for him not coming immediately, all he needs is a bit more training; don't beat him!' I am pleased to say that I never did see him beat his dog again, so hopefully what I said gave him food for thought.

There never seems to be an end to all the situations which can be connected with the recall and the various problems which owners have with the exercise. Sooner or later they present these problems to their instructors who really have to scratch their heads

at times to work out the easiest and most effective ways of dealing with them. And when they have, it is then up to the owners to work on them.

I was once asked in a television interview whether one could get a 100 per cent success when correcting problems with dogs. I replied that regrettably no, it was not possible. There are two main reasons for this; firstly when problems have manifested themselves for far too long, and secondly when owners just have not got what it takes to correct the problem even though the dog might respond to an experienced trainer.

Only a year or so ago a lady bought a Dobermann, which was at least 4 years old, to me. Her husband had trained him in an obedience dog club and he had done all the basic exercises, including the recall. The couple later separated and the dog remained with her, but unfortunately proved to be rather a problem.

First of all, he would continuously try to push her out of the way when doing heelwork! However, it took only 2 weeks to correct that problem by doing lots of left turns and left-about turns which had the effect of cutting off the dog's advance by stepping very quickly around in front of him so many times. This eventually made him drop back to the proper heel position whereby he could not push her over to the right with his shoulder. But the recall exercise during free running presented a greater problem. If she told the dog to 'Sit' and 'Stay', she could walk away many metres, turn around and face the dog, call him, and he would come immediately, sit perfectly straight in front and do a perfect finish to heel. But as soon as she let the dog off for a free run and tried to call him, he would not come at all. He would play around for at least half an hour; it proved to be a waste of time going after him to catch him, it was impossible. He would let you get within a few metres of him and then dash off again and, as you know, when that breed moves it moves very fast. All the usual methods of running in the opposite direction, falling down on the ground and all those sorts of things failed to get any response. You just had to wait until he came back and then put him on the lead again. The check cord method was used, but without any success.

After several weeks I had to explain to this lady that there was no point in going on. He was 4 years old, and although he could do a perfect recall in a trial ring situation he was that smart in knowing that he could get away with it at any other time.

You may wonder what had gone wrong in the dog's training. Well, the answer is quite simple. The dog had been trained by her husband to do the recall under trial conditions only and not in various situations when free walking and free running. Had that been done when he was a puppy or very young dog, I am quite sure that he would have responded at any time. But we had to concede that it was too late at the age of 4 years to do anything about it.

Had I had the dog myself all the time, possibly I could have got through to it, but I have my doubts in view of the fact that he had been getting away with this for 4 years.

Therefore we had to admit that that dog was virtually incurable of this particular problem.

The reason why I mention this story is to make you aware of how this fault in training can develop into a major problem. So, when you call your dog, don't just do the recall as you would expect to do it in a trial ring, but do it under all circumstances, so that your dog will come at any time.

At about the same time a young 12-year-old girl, who lived in the local milk bar, brought a beautiful German Shepherd dog to me for training, and I must say she learnt extremely well. I found her to be a very conscientious young lady. She had very quick reflexes, and coming from a German family she was very industrious.

We taught the dog the basic exercises including the recall and we had reached the stage of teaching the dog to come during free running in the local park adjacent to Melbourne's Yarra River. And then one day after he had done quite a few recalls, he went down to the river and swam across the strong flowing current and climbed up on to the opposite bank. Despite our calls he just sat there and looked at us, which was most annoying.

I knew the only way to get over to him was to drive at least 6km (4 miles) round to the nearest bridge downstream, or 6km via another bridge upstream. I also knew that by the time I had reached him he might well have swum back to the young girl. So what was I to do?

I just had to think of some devious means of attracting him. Now dogs know when other dogs are in distress, just like birds and other animals will know when their species are in distress; they have that wonderful instinctive means of communication. A dog barks in many ways, when it is joyful, when it is threatened, suspicious or aggressive, when it is lonely and bored, or in various other moods, and at the same time we, as humans, can tell by the tone of the bark what sort of mood the dog is in.

So I crept down through the bushes and trees to the nearer bank, and made a noise like a puppy or young dog in distress! Having been brought up with dogs, having seen some dogs in distress and having, I suppose, a way of imitating them, it wasn't very hard for me to do this. As soon as I started howling I saw him prick up his ears and show great interest. He stood there for a moment, and then dived into the river and swam strongly across that current to get to me. He could not see me because I was in the bushes, but he could hear the sounds of the distressed dog that I was imitating.

As he was crossing the river, I anticipated that as soon as he saw who it was he might either run past me or go back into the river again and swim back to the opposite bank. I therefore had to think of something which would still attract his curiosity, so as he was getting to the river bank I started scratching the ground as if there was something on the ground making this noise! He came out of the water and came straight up to me and put his nose right down to the ground where I was scratching, whereby I was able to take hold of him by the collar in the other hand, and clip on the leash and follow through with the recall.

Yes, I guess you can say I had to think up a crafty method on the spur of the moment. As I did, I recalled the words Sandon Moss once said to me, 'When you are dealing with a crafty dog you must be doubly crafty!'

A couple of days later we took the girl's dog down to the park near the river again and put him on a long check cord. As we expected, he tried to go in the river again. But only once, whereupon I gave him the command, 'No', and a very firm jerk on the cord from about 6m (20ft) away, which caught him by surprise, and he soon got the message that he was not allowed to go into the river and swim to the other side. I am pleased to say that he never ran away again.

A little while ago a young fellow came to me with a beautiful Dalmatian dog. He was a very wilful dog, and as you can imagine he had a load of initiative. He had no fears or aggression, and generally speaking had a very nice temperament. But he certainly was a little devil. Once he got off the lead he just would not come back. He was full of mischief!

Anyway, we set about training him, and within two or three lessons we had taught him to heel, sit and stay, and to come on the leash. Sometimes he would come, other times he would just take off, and when running free in a huge area, he just would not come back. We had to go after him again, and again, and again. And after a while I could see that he was just losing more and more respect for his owner.

Now when dogs lose respect like this in the recall, I have found the best way of correcting them and showing the owner what to do is to put the dog on the leash and do some very fast and intensive heelwork in order to get respect again and quickly. So I took this Dalmatian and gave him some heelwork, which included about two right turns, a right-about turn and about four sits. I did all that within about 12 seconds. The dog just didn't realise what had happened to him. And neither did the owner, he had never seen a dog put through its paces so quickly in so short a time. I then did the recall on the leash, and then let the dog off the leash, and within 2 or 3 seconds as he was running away I recalled him sharply, and he turned completely round and came straight back to me at top speed and sat, perfectly straight and still. The young man could not believe it. He found it hard to understand how the dog could be so naughty, and then within half a minute he was doing perfect recalls. As I pointed out what had actually happened in that case and cases like it, was that the dog had lost more and more respect for him and found out that he could get away with it at any time and just run off. By suddenly putting in a burst of heelwork like that, respect is restored, and then straight into a recall on the leash, followed immediately with a recall in free running. Once an owner has seen this training technique he is then able to do it himself when the need arises. And that certainly did happen. Later on in the lesson, the dog dashed off again and it was about 2 minutes before he was caught. Now the young man knew exactly what to do and carried out the quick piece of heelwork just like I had shown him; 'Heel', 'Sit', 'Heel', 'Sit', 'Heel', 'Sit', a couple of turns, then the recalls, 'Come; good boy'. The dog responded perfectly, showing great respect and willingness.

The following week when he came for training his work was excellent. The week after we took him to another park where there were lots of dogs running around, and we tested him out, and let him go after the other dogs and play with them. When called, he came back immediately. On other occasions we let him run after the other dogs, and when he was about halfway or three-quarters of the way towards them, he came back immediately when called.

The young man was so pleased. He said, 'I can go anywhere now, run my Dalmatian and he will always come back immediately'. The dog's performance was so good that I tried to encourage the young man to go on and join a dog club and go in for obedience trials, because his dog certainly had the makings for that particular type of work. But unfortunately, and of course it was the owner's decision, he had no intention of going in for obedience trials; all he wanted was a well-behaved dog. Well, that was his prerogative. But I knew, only too well, that there must be some people in dog clubs who would have given anything to have had a dog like that, with which they could have gone on to work in obedience trials.

Some of the naughtiest dogs you can find are dogs which have high degrees of initiative and, when trained, that initiative is not destroyed, but channelled in the right direction. This makes the dog a fantastic worker. So don't despair if you have a naughty dog, you should welcome it really.

Although you may find it hard to train it, you can end up with a brilliant worker.

About 10 years ago, when the Old English Sheepdog seemed to be very popular in Victoria, a young man brought one along to me for basic training. Both he and the dog did extremely well in the first few weeks. Their heelwork was a pleasure to watch. The dog stayed well and was very quick when recalled on the leash or off the leash at a short distance. However, a problem arose when he was recalled during free running. He would hear the command to come, but would then run off in different directions, and had to be called many times until he finally came and sat in front of his owner.

At first sight one would have thought that the dog was just playing around, but this was not so in this case. The reason for the many deviations he made when recalled was because he had so much hair over his eyes, which made it hard for him to see where his master was. Sometimes on that particular ground where we were calling the dog, his master's voice echoed against certain walls and buildings, and although the dog was obviously doing his best, he was confused about the real direction from where the command was being uttered.

Now it so happened that this young man had no intention of showing the dog at all; he just wanted the dog to be an obedient pet. So I asked him if he would mind cutting away some of the hair around the dog's eyes so that he could see clearly. It is a fallacy actually to think that if you cut the hair away from an Old English Sheepdog's eyes it will go blind. However, you only need cut enough hair away so that the dog can see, leaving a little umbrella effect above his eyes so as to act as a shade against the bright sunlight.

He duly trimmed the hair around his dog's eyes and when he came for his final lesson the following week, he had no trouble at all when he recalled his dog during free running. The dog responded immediately every time. He came in fast and straight and thoroughly enjoyed it.

So if you have an Old English Sheepdog, or a breed which has long hair over the eyes, it is advisable to keep the hair trimmed if you do not intend to show the dog. If you do show your dog, then you can always pin up its hair effectively with some form of hair grip or even a coloured ribbon tied in a bow which will make it look pretty at the same time!

5 Difficult Dogs

When people contact me and tell me all about the problems they are having with their dogs, I can really understand how they feel. I know how frustrated and anxious they have become over the many months they have tried in vain to deal with their dogs. At the same time I know exactly how most of the problems have been caused and promoted, but must admit that there are a few problems which are very difficult to work out. While most people are very good in supplying relevant information concerning the behaviour of their dogs, a few seem to either withhold certain details or do not think it is necessary to supply them. I cannot therefore really work out the problem until I actually see the dog and observe how the owner handles it.

I am always happy to say that in the vast majority of cases the cause can be worked out and what has appeared to be a real problem at first sight is soon cured when the owner is shown how to correct it and prevent it occurring again. This naturally comes as a welcome surprise, for many owners think they have possibly reached the stage whereby it is too late to do anything. Unfortunately there are some cases which have been left too late, and I have mentioned a few of these in this book.

A few years ago a young lady phoned me up and told me she had been going to a dog club for several months with her Boxer bitch. She had made no progress whatsoever, the dog was highly excitable and had learnt nothing. Then she was told by a group of the instructors in that obedience club that they considered her dog was untrainable.

This of course upset the young lady, but at the same time she was determined to do something about it. It was her pet dog, and all she wanted was just basic training. She wanted to be able to go out and have the dog walking at heel, to sit, to stay and come when she called her, and to generally behave herself. That was all she wanted.

She told me the whole story, and I made an appointment for her to bring her dog to see me. When they arrived we drove to a local park. We got out and walked on to the grass where I asked her, 'Well, what I would like you to do first is to do what you can; what you have been taught. Just a bit of heelwork, a sit, two or three turns, and we will see what happens'.

So she brought the dog to heel, sat her, and then started off. Well, I've never seen a person walk so quickly, and when she did of course the dog was highly excited. It just kept on jumping up, like a yo-yo! And when she jumped, she jumped up as high as the handler's head height. The dog was highly excited when she did turns, and would not sit when told. She jumped around all over the place. It seemed hopeless trying to get the dog to lie down. And as some would see it, the dog was untrainable. But the cause of the trouble in this case was that the girl was walking far too quickly. This I must add was not really her fault. She had been told to walk quickly in the class, and keep up with all the others. Now with an excitable dog this is one thing you just do not do.

So I took the dog and showed her how to walk slowly, how to sit her properly, how to heel her properly and how to stroke her and talk to her very calmly and quietly. 'Stroke it very slowly and very gently,' I said, 'never pat the dog or stroke it quickly, otherwise it will jump up or move in excitement'.

In that first lesson the dog calmed right down and the young lady went home much happier. During the next week she just taught her dog to go forward, to heel, to sit and also do a right-about turn. During the following week I spent the first few minutes watching her carry out the very simple heelwork I recommended that she should practise a little each day, and I was very pleased with the results. She had obviously carried out my instructions very well and was very happy with the pleasing results she had attained with the dog.

In the second lesson she learnt how to turn left and right and to teach the dog to sit and stay. In the third lesson we taught the dog to come on the lead; in the fourth lesson we taught the dog to come off the lead. And then we started doing free running and taught the dog to lie down as well. So in about seven or eight lessons we had completed the dog's basic training, and I might add that after a few lessons we were able to very gradually increase her speed of walking.

Now towards the end of the time this young lady was so thrilled that her dog could do all these things, that she joined another obedience dog club so that she could at least get her dog to walk among other dogs, and this had my full support. She had some fantastic results, they really were excellent.

Then one day, she phoned me and said, 'I understand they have what they call obedience trials, and I would very much like to enter one of them. Could you continue to train me, and give me coaching in this direction?' I said that I would be very happy to do this and she came again for a further series of training lessons, and I explained to her what was required in the obedience trials. To cut a long story short, she trained consistently and when she could do all the Novice work, she entered for the trials, and before long she earned her first obedience title — Companion Dog (CD).

She then came back and said, 'I would like to go higher!' So I trained her for the Open, which of course includes the broad jump, high jump and retrieving, stays out of sight, and drop on recall. And before long she was awarded her next title — Companion Dog Excellent (CDX).

Immediately she got this she came back again and said, 'I understand they also do what is called "tracking". Could I come on one of your tracking courses?' And so I took her on a tracking course, and before long she competed in a tracking trial and got her Tracking Dog title (TD).

I understand she went on for Utility work but her dog met with a slight accident which strained its back and it was felt best to retire her from competitive work. There was a case of a dog which had been certified 'untrainable', but when the owner was shown how to train and work with her properly, they achieved great success together.

Untrainable dog? Never in your life! That dog had great potential and it proves that if a dog is trained properly it will repay in many ways. It had a load of spirit, stamina and a tremendous willingness to please. And not only did it thrive on work, but it had such a lovely friendly character, in fact it was quite a comic at times and enjoyed every bit of life.

Several years ago a gentleman phoned me up to tell me that he had a German Shepherd cross, and when he came home the dog would sometimes bite him lightly on the leg, and at other times when he was fast asleep in an armchair, the dog, without any warning at all, would jump and attack him by biting him on the chest. He said that the dog was highly excitable, and appeared to be quite a neurotic case.

I listened for some time, because in listening to a client on the telephone I can obtain a lot of information rather than by just asking questions. As he spoke, I considered that in this particular case it would be necessary for me to go to his home to see this dog and the relationship which the dog had with him and with the rest of his family in the home. And so after a while I offered to visit him, and he accepted my offer with great appreciation.

When I visited his home and met him and his wife, the dog was outside in the back garden. We spoke for at least half an hour, during which time I could tell that the gentleman was very tense indeed. He spoke very loudly and very quickly. Anyway, I asked him if he would like to go out and bring his dog in from the garden, so that I could observe its behaviour inside.

While he was outside calling the dog, I quickly turned to his wife and said, 'Your husband is very tense, what sort of work does he do?' She told me that he was a foreman in a factory, he had a responsible position and he had about 50 men under him. I asked her, 'Is it a noisy factory?' to which she replied, 'Yes, it is'. And so I said, 'Well, I assume then that when he speaks to the men he must have to raise his voice'. 'Yes, this is quite true', she explained, 'So that they can hear him over the noise of the machinery'.

The dog was brought in, and I found

it to be quite friendly as it greeted me for the first time, but I could also tell that, being a sensitive dog, he could be easily upset if he was shouted at, and that was the sort of thing that had been happening when his master came home from work each day.

The following week they came over to my house for training. Apart from teaching him how to heel the dog, sit the dog and do the turns, the greatest thing I had to work on was to get the man to relax and to talk very quietly to his dog. I had to whisper and ask him to copy my whispering voice. Now for a lot of people who speak very loudly it is not easy for them to suddenly change and calm down and talk quietly. So I told him to imagine that there was a baby fast asleep in a pram in every front garden he passed, and that when he gave a command to his dog he should say it firmly to have the desired effect on his dog, but at the same time it must not be said too loudly so as to wake the baby. This method I have often used with people, and sure enough it works. It is amazing how you can give a stern command in a whisper!

I am pleased to say that this gentleman improved lesson by lesson, and as he improved of course his dog improved, and as they progressed they learned more exercises. Around about the eighth lesson he was free running his dog in the local park, allowing it to run off and play with other dogs and, when he called it, it came to him immediately. And so in those 2 months he had achieved much and was very happy with the results.

But the interesting thing about that case was that during the last lesson his wife turned to me, as he was about 100m away working the dog, and said, 'My husband is a different man now. Since he has been coming to train, you have taught him how to relax, be calm and very quiet, and now when he comes in he does so very slowly, shuts the door and talks quietly and slowly, and sits down. He does not dash around and start shouting like he used to. And then later on he takes the dog out for a walk and this helps him to relax. He feels that he can get completely away from his work and just go out and enjoy a nice stroll with the dog which is more relaxed and much better behaved. The dog has not bitten my husband again and is not frustrated like he used to be'. That is one of many stories in which you could so rightly say, 'They all lived happily ever after'.

I had a phone call from a family who had an 18-months-old Afghan hound. They had him since he was 4 months of age. Although they had tried they found it hopeless to take him out for a walk because he just would not walk! He would just lie down, and show his stubbornness. They tried dragging him, but still he would not walk. Finally they were more or less forced to pick him up and carry him. They had tried everything they knew, but obviously they had not been firm enough. So an appointment was made, and a few days later they arrived. As it had been a very hot day, about 38°C (100°F), I was training in the cool of the evening. The car pulled up and watching from my lounge window I saw them carry this huge dog with a flowing shaggy coat up my drive, up the steps, and put him down outside my front door. I went out and met the family — mother and father and three grown-up girls — and we talked while the dog just stood there and looked down its long nose!

After some minutes, I took the lead and said, 'Let's go for a little walk' and just beckoned the dog and said 'Come along then' and sure enough the dog followed me down the steps and down the drive. But just as we passed the car, down he went, and by the look on his face was quite adamant that he was not going to go any further. He had actually walked that far because he thought he was going to go back to the car.

And so I said 'Come along', gave him a jerk, and proceeded to walk straight on up the road. Then it happened — didn't he let out a cry! A cry of utter annoyance! Nobody had ever made him do it before, and he decided that he was certainly going to create a scene about it. As he cried, screamed, battled and reared up on his hind legs like a wild stallion, I decided right there and then I was not going to stop, but that I was going to walk straight on up the road, without any hesitation. I told myself, as I tell all my clients to tell themselves, that I was going to win, and that he was going to be quiet eventually. And so one of the daughters came with me, as he cried all the way up the road for about 300m (330 yd). During this time of course neighbours, who were gardening in their front gardens, looked up in astonishment at the way he was carrying on. It was either him or me! And it wasn't going to be me who was going to be the loser!

However, after 330m (¼ mile) he decided to give in and walk, and as soon as he started to respond in this way, I praised him. We walked on for about half a kilometre, towards the end of which not only was he walking well on a loose leash, but he was wagging his tail, and thoroughly enjoying it! I then handed the leash to the girl and she walked him all the way back to my house without any trouble at all. In fact, the rest of the family, who were sitting in their car awaiting our return, just could not believe their eyes when they saw their own dog walking along so happily.

Now when I gave the family last-minute instructions as they departed that evening, I told them that this trouble might happen again, and if it did they should not worry, but deal with his stubbornness quite firmly as I had done. I quite expected this trouble to happen the next day, or even for the next 2 or 3 days, especially when they were in their own home area.

However, the following week when they came for the second lesson I inquired as to how they had been getting on, and whether or not their Afghan had shown any more stubbornness. They were highly delighted to say that he had changed completely and that he had come to thoroughly enjoy going out for walks even from the point when they took his leash out of the drawer, and not once had he shown any more stubbornness as he had shown for 14 months.

Some time later another very stubborn Afghan was brought to me. He was about 12 months old and flatly refused to go for a walk. His owner told me that when she tried to make him walk on the leash he would rear up on his hind legs and wrap his front legs around the leash, scream and become very aggressive by trying to bite the leash.

When he came to my place he was quite happy. In fact he appeared to be a very affectionate dog and enjoyed being stroked as we stood and talked in the street. But as soon as he was invited to come for a walk, he rebelled. Even when I tugged forward on the leash he immediately dug his feet into the ground and refused to budge. I gave him another tug on the leash and as quick as lightning he jumped up and wrapped both his front paws over the leash and locked them tightly together and started snarling and snapping. Normally I try to untangle the leash from a dog's front paws, but I knew that in this case if I attempted to do that he would surely bite me. Whether he would bite intentionally or not, you could not say for certain, but I would say that he would have just bitten anyone or anything that happened to be in his way.

So I just pulled on the leash, and he walked on his hind legs, snarling and snapping. I reckoned that if I kept on walking, eventually he would wear himself out and cease to rebel. Sure enough he did. But I don't mind admitting that I was quite exhausted after that encounter, but pleased to say that after about 500m he just suddenly stopped and stood there. I relaxed the tension on the leash and beckoned him to walk along with me. This he did immediately and I gave him sincere praise and from that point on he was quite all right.

The owner, who was walking beside me, then took over, and we had no more trouble. We did not teach the dog to heel, or do anything else that day. The important thing was to get him to walk happily on the leash. Giving lavish praise, it was not long before he really enjoyed the walk and started to wag his tail.

From that day on the lady had no more trouble with him and in subsequent weeks we taught him basic heelwork, the stay and recall.

Both these cases of extreme stubbornness started off by the two dogs just wanting to have their own way. The trouble developed because their respective owners did not exercise enough authority over their hounds; instead they gave in when they started howling their heads off in the street. In a very short time dogs like these will soon find out that if they create a scene which can be embarrassing, their owners will cease to make them do what they want them to do. Basically the two cases are the same, but the reactions of each dog, when made to walk, are slightly different. It is also interesting to note that the results were the same. Although these two cases concern Afghan hounds, stubbornness can of course be found in many breeds of dogs. Many people think that Afghan hounds are stupid dogs. On the contrary, they are very clever. True, they are not easy to train and I think these two stories clearly illustrate how difficult they can be.

Just to show that there can be various causes for the same sort of problem, I well remember a lady who purchased an Australian Terrier at the age of 9 months. He was a lovely little fellow, but had never been walked on a leash. When the lady tried to lead him on a leash, even within her own back garden, the little dog just froze and crumpled up. No matter how much she encouraged him, he would not move. She brought the dog to me and he did exactly the same when I tried to get him to walk. He was not stubborn, but just frightened. No amount of praise and encouragement would entice him to even walk a couple of steps. I blamed this entirely on the breeder who had kept him for the 9 months; hoping, like many breeders do, that he would develop into a good show dog. In all that time the breeder admitted that she had never put the puppy on a light leash. In consequence, when he had been introduced to leash walking in his new home, it was too much of a shock to his system.

Now although I do not believe in the use of food in training dogs, except of course when training puppies to come when they are between 6 to 10 weeks of age, I decided to make an exception in this particular case. Having him on a very light slack leash, we enticed him along a few centimetres at a time with little pieces of meat. This worked and he gained confidence in the first lesson, and I advised the lady to do it again the next day at her home. This she did and gave her little dog plenty of praise as he responded. After that he never needed a food incentive again. He walked along very happily as she gave him plenty of praise. The main point I wish to make here is that there are exceptional times and places where you might have to resort to using food, but in so doing it should only be used for a very, very short time in order to get the initial response. From then on the reward should be replaced with sincere praise given by voice and hand. If food is continued for longer, it is likely that the dog will only respond when food is present and not at other times.

6 Clever Dogs

You hear many people complain about their dogs and the reasons are usually because they have problems with them. Some go on to criticise everything about their dogs and you wonder why on earth they got them in the first place. But you will usually find that owners who are like this tend to complain about more or less everything in life. I always think that it is a great pity when people don't learn to notice and cherish all the good things that surround them, and adopt a positive attitude by attempting to put right the things which appear to be wrong. This also applies when caring for and living with dogs.

It is always very pleasing to me when I hear dog owners give great credit to their dogs, even if they are a bit naughty, and to marvel at their cleverness.

One of the first things that they notice about their dogs is that, after about the second time they come for training, the dog knows, within about a quarter of a kilometre of my training school, where it is going and shows this by becoming quite excited in the car. They also notice how their dogs like coming for training. One classic example was of a Bouvier de Flanders which came regularly once a week. When the lady and her husband arrived on the sixth time, they got the bitch, who was naturally very pleased to see me, out of the car and we chatted for about a couple of minutes. Because everything was going extremely well I decided that we should drive, for the first time, to a local park and work the dog there. The couple had been looking forward to this and so turned around and took the dog back to their car. But then there arose a problem which they had never experienced before — the dog refused to get in the car! What she wanted to do was to go into my place to do some training like she had done before over the past 5 weeks. Anyway, with great effort they eventually got her into the car and we drove to the park. There she worked beautifully: heeled well, did her stays, had free runs and came every time she was called. Then she got into the car quite happily and sat there with a look on her face as much as to say, 'I enjoyed that workout!' We all had a good laugh about it, as it was quite obvious to all of us that previously outside my house she thought she was going to miss out on her training session!

I must tell you of another interesting thing which happens from time to time, and that is that dogs get to know my name. It is also interesting to note that it is nearly always German Shepherds which excel themselves in this way.

First they come for one lesson, and then the next time they come the owners tell me that their dogs get quite excited when they actually turn into the road and they have only about 200m (220yd) to go. The dogs know, by their sense of smell, where they are and associate it with coming for training. And then perhaps in the third lesson the dogs indicate this earlier, even when they are about half a kilometre or more away. This excitement clearly shows how they come to enjoy training.

Some of these people have actually used my name when they have been coming along, even as soon as they have left their homes. One young lady used to say to her dog, 'Now we are going to see Uncle Mike today; yes, Uncle Mike'. And as she went along in the car, she would say, 'Yes, going to see Uncle Mike' and the dog built up an association of 'Uncle Mike' and coming for training. Other people have said 'Mr Tucker', and others have just said 'Michael'.

Going back to this dog who knew me as Uncle Mike, whenever he was misbehaving at home during the week his owner would say, 'I'll take you to Uncle Mike, he'll sort you out! Take you to Uncle Mike!' and as soon as she mentioned my name the dog

behaved himself. Now this is not surprising because the dog had associated my name with training and having to do as he was told.

Another case, and this once again was a German Shepherd, was where a lady had been coming to me for some time and had always refered to me as Mr Tucker to the dog. One day she was entertaining some friends in her lounge, and her dog was misbehaving a little bit. One of her friends said, 'Do you still take your dog to training?' She replied, 'Yes,' and then her friend asked 'To whom do you go?' The lady said, 'A man called Michael Tucker' and as soon as the dog heard my name he behaved himself.

There have been scores of cases where people, who have been coming to me for training, have mentioned after having had a few lessons that they have noticed that their dogs have behaved much better in my local district than they have in their respective home areas.

They are of course quite right in their observations and while it does not happen with most dogs, it is to be expected with those which are known to be naughty and clever. There are three main reasons why these particular dogs work better when they come for a lesson. Firstly, I am instructing each owner in what to say to the dog and how to say it; also what to do and the best way in how to control the dog physically and how to anticipate and prevent the dog doing the wrong things. When the owner is receiving all this help the chance of anything going wrong is minimal, whereas when they are practising in their home districts during the week as conscientiously as they might, they may use the wrong tone of voice, give an ineffective physical correction, be too slow in giving a word of reproof, forget to give praise at the right time, and not having the experience and enough understanding of the dog's intentions and reactions so as to prevent faults occurring.

Secondly, each dog soon learns to associate the area in my district as being a place where it has to behave and do as it is told. To extend this I try to use different streets, my own back garden, the local shopping areas and finally the local parks.

Thirdly, and most important of all, I have a dual role as dog trainer and instructor. With every dog which comes to me for basic training, I always handle it and give it some training first, and at the same time show the owner, who walks along on my right-hand side, what to do. After a little while I hand the dog over to the owner and instruct and help the owner to train his or her dog. I use this procedure with every exercise. Naturally, the dog very soon learns to respect me as trainer. In most cases he learns to respect me more than his owner. That is to be expected, of course. But in time, with continued instruction and provided the owner trains the dog conscientiously, the dog should learn to respect the owner as well as, if not better than, me as the trainer who actually gave the dog its initial training in every exercise.

In contrast to this, dogs which attend obedience dog training clubs, where the instructors for various reasons do not handle the dogs but instead just stand out in front of a class and give instructions, do not have that same respect for the class instructors.

I always find it interesting and somewhat amusing when owners tell me how their dogs have played up during the week and from what they tell me I know what to expect. So I tell them not to worry as we start off in the next lesson. I may walk about 2 metres (2yd) away from the dog, while the owner works the dog in heelwork with the occasional sit-stay and recall on the leash as we walk down the road. The dog works so well that the owner exclaims, 'Well, would you believe it, my dog is making a liar out of me!' 'Please don't worry!' I assure the owner, 'I know that what you say has happened during the last week is quite true'. As they proceed forward again I move away and walk on the other side of the road, whereupon the dog starts to misbehave in various ways; after a short distance I gradually cross the road again to be nearer to them. The dog sees me come closer and obeys every word its owner commands. After a little while I gradually move away again. The dog notices my position and plays up again! I then move closer to them and the dog obeys every command. During the entire part of that walk I have neither given a command to the dog, nor have I touched it. It has obeyed the owner because it has respected my presence as I have walked in fairly close proximity to them, but disobeyed the owner when I have drifted away to the other side of the road.

It is certainly a clever dog which can do this and although it is somewhat frustrating for the owner in these early days, it is amusing to see the changing expressions on the dog's face! When the dog is trying to get away with everything you can see a cheeky type of grin all over its face. As I walk closer to it, the expression changes to quite a serious one as it concentrates and walks willingly. Dogs are just like naughty children at times. When owners see that their dogs can perform really well, it does, I feel, give them confidence in at least knowing that their dogs are capable of doing the exercises and they are not untrainable dogs, as they might first have imagined. They then realise that with more hard work they will achieve these good results when they are on their own with their dogs.

I shall always remember a special case when a young lady came to me with her very clever 6-months-old German Shepherd. He had a lot of initiative and because of that you can imagine how naughty he was. Anyway he trained well, but one day after several weekly lessons she told me that while he would work well in my local park, he would always play up on her in her local park, which was some kilometres away.

So she asked me if I could manage to visit her home area and observe them work together. I agreed to do this and we arranged a time and date and the place where we would meet. I told her that I would sit in my car which I would park so that the wind, if any, was blowing from where she was going to work him towards my car, so that he could not possibly wind-scent me.

So on the arranged day I drove to her local park, and having checked out the wind direction took up my posi-tion and waited. At the appointed time I saw her walk into the park and she went through all the exercises: heel-work, turns, stand, sit, drop, stay and recall. In every single exercise her dog misbehaved, just as she had told me he would do. He sniffed, he was dis-tracted towards other dogs and people who walked through the park, he walked wide on their turns, would not always sit, he got up in his drops, would not always stay and would not always come when called.

After about 12 minutes or so, I got out of my car and casually walked over to the edge of the park and then all of a sudden when I was about 30 metres away from them, he saw me. The immediate expression on that dog's face was one of complete as-tonishment, so much so that if he could have spoken he would have said, 'Good gracious, what on earth are you doing here? I didn't expect you to turn up here on my own training ground!' I found it so interesting to watch him from then on because from the instant he spotted me he obeyed every com-mand his owner gave. I did not in-tervene. There was no need. I neither said a word nor did I move from where I stood. She took him through all the exercises again, which he did per-fectly. I am happy to say that like so many conscientious handlers she stuck at it and by her determination she got the results she set out to achieve.

About a year after that I had a very similar case. This time it was with a Standard Schnauzer which was owned by a very nice elderly lady in her eighties. She was an extremely active person for her age, for she even went swimming every morning and went skiing overseas whenever she could. Her dog had a delightful character, but like lots of other clever dogs he could be very naughty. While I was around he would obey her and work very well, but even when she brought him to my local park when I was not around he would misbehave. So one morning I arranged for her to bring him to my local park so that I could observe his behaviour. I arrived there well before they did and positioned myself so that he could not possibly wind-scent me. I sat in my car and watched from a distance, and sure enough he misbehaved a lot. He knew perfectly well what to do, but was still determined to have his own way. After about 10 minutes I got out of my car and walked across and stood by a thick fence post. Although he could not wind-scent me I knew that sooner or later he was bound to see me and sure

enough he did. From that point on he obeyed every word she said. And nearly every time she gave him a command he would glance quickly at me, as much as to say, 'Are you still watching me?' She would let him have a free run and then recall him, to which he came immediately and sat perfectly straight and close in front of her, and would then give a quick glance over his shoulder at me, with an expression on his face which said, 'There now, aren't I clever?'

So there are two stories, two of many which illustrate the fact that dogs definitely know when an instructor or a person who has actually trained them is watching from a distance. The respect is still there even though the dogs do not totally respect their owners, and they obey their commands because the instructor, whom they do respect, is in that vicinity.

7 Fear in Dogs

You often hear people say that their dog is frightened of something or other, but don't always know how it became frightened in the first place or why it should be like that. They are at a loss to know how they can help their dog get over its fear or what can be done. After a while most owners are resigned to the fact that it is too late to do anything about it. So much depends on the type of fear the dog has, how and when it was caused, the type of environment and conditions in which the dog lives, the daily routine it leads and the various places to which the dog is taken.

There are four main types of fear in dogs. They are *nervousness, sound shyness, suspicion* and *anxiety.* They can all be seen in varying degrees and there are a number of ways by which they are unfortunately caused. Pure nervousness is simply an ailment of the brain and is the result of bad breeding. There is no known cure and, quite frankly, I believe the kindest thing to do with a dog with this trait is to have it painlessly destroyed.

Fortunately, cases of pure nervousness are rare, but I recall one case which was brought to me a few years ago by two very nice ladies. Because it was a very sad case I think it needs mentioning to illustrate this terrible trait. The dog was a German Shepherd bitch and she was in a terrible and hopeless state. I did all I could to calm and control her but to no avail. She tried to dash here, there and everywhere. She continuously cried, and had the shakes. No way could I get through to her. The two ladies who cared for her had obviously done all they possibly could have done for her. After I had spent a fair time in observing and handling her, my advice was that they had her put to sleep. They faced the situation quite sensibly and took my advice which was supported by their vet.

Occasionally you come across a dog which is sound shy — also known as a gun-shy dog. This is where a dog is frightened by loud and unexpected noises which affect its sense of hearing. The trait can either be inherited or it can develop any time in puppyhood or adulthood if, over a period of time, the dog has been subjected to continuous loud noises.

When I was a boy, we had a Fox Terrier which became terrified when she heard the roar of a motor bike or the loud cracks of a thunder storm. She would remain in a state of trembling and panting for between 1 and 2 hours after the event. But, despite this unfortunate trait, which was considered to be hereditary, she lived to the good age of 14 years.

I have known of a few cases of guide dogs which, although they had passed all their rigorous tests during their initial testing time and 4 months of training, suddenly developed sound shyness several months after they had been successfully working with their new owners — the blind people. Some of the cases were where the dogs were working every day in extremely noisy city conditions; other cases were where the guide dogs were accommodated near the work benches of their owners in very noisy factories. Nowadays, guide dog organisations carefully look into these conditions beforehand and advise and negotiate with the managements to provide suitable accommodation for the guide dogs. It should be sufficiently far away from the actual factory building for the dog to be able to rest comfortably and not be subjected to loud industrial noises, and so prevent the development of sound shyness.

If a dog has more than a small degree of sound shyness it is virtually impossible to cure. If a dog has a minute degree, there is always a slim chance of getting the dog over sound shyness by conditioning it to very mild noises at first. This must be done very carefully and over a long period of time.

Suspicion is a natural trait in all dogs, in fact, there is no dog without it. Even the boldest dogs can show a little bit of suspicion by backing away and then gradually coming up to a very strange looking person or thing which they have not seen before or are not too sure about. But any more than a little bit of suspicion is an undesirable trait in working dogs such as guide dogs, police dogs and dogs used in other services.

Dogs can be suspicious of all sorts of things — men, women, children, dogs, cats and other animals; traffic and odd looking things in the streets; things high up like moving cranes; and just about anything you like to name.

Why are dogs suspicious? And what can cause this trait? In most cases it is where the dog during its puppyhood has not been walked regularly in order to condition and socialise it to everything in the outside world. And even when this has been carried out properly, dogs can still show suspicion towards particular people, animals or things if they have had an unfortunate and unpleasant experience when making contact with them in the past.

These suspicions, provided they are mild, can be cured with careful handling and conditioning. It is a case of getting the dog confident in the handler, and for the handler to instil confidence in the dog. This should be done by carefully and patiently introducing it to all those things to which it has shown suspicion, so that it builds up in its mind a good association of ideas. Naturally this takes time, but it is so necessary if you want to have a dog with a sound temperament.

People often ask, 'Can dogs learn to do something by copying another dog?' The answer to this is, 'Yes, they can', but the things which they copy are those which are seen in the natural and instinctive acts of behaviour in dogs. These include chasing, barking, digging holes and many others. Unfortunately they are always the things you don't want them to do.

Instinctive behaviour is natural, but training is artificial. It is designed by humans, if you like. It is something which has to be kept up or otherwise the dog will revert to its natural state.

You cannot therefore demonstrate with a fully-trained dog and expect other dogs to learn to do the same by watching it perform the exercises! It would be very nice if you could, but you cannot!

If a dog is allowed to roam outside its owner's property, there is no knowing what it might get up to. One of the bad traits it might develop is to chase cars, and if other dogs are in the company of a car chaser they are likely to copy the trait, which can be positively dangerous to both motorists and dogs. Worse still is a dog which takes to chasing sheep and then goes one step further and starts killing them. Once again, other dogs which accompany it are highly likely to do the same.

In a large kennel environment where there are a number of dogs, if one starts digging in a grass exercise yard, others will do likewise. And a most undesirable trait is where a dog takes to eating its own or other dogs' motions. If this is not stopped promptly, this filthy habit will be copied by other dogs.

This brings me to explain how a puppy or young dog can actually copy the reactions of a suspicious dog with which it is unfortunately kennelled. I well remember one particular Chihuahua puppy which was brought to me for temperamental assessment and basic training for the show ring. He was 4½ months of age at the time and he had a general suspicion of people and various things. I asked the owner, who was also the breeder, if she still had him kennelled with his mother. She said that he was and that she also walked him every day with her. I then asked what the mother's temperament was like, to which she replied, 'Well, she is a little bit suspicious too!' 'That accounts for it,' I explained, 'that is why the puppy is suspicious — he is copying her'. I then asked, 'Do you by any chance happen to own the sire, or does he belong to someone else?' 'Yes, as a matter of fact I do own him,' she explained, 'and his temperament is quite the opposite — he's as bold as brass!' 'In that case,' I advised, 'if you wish to walk your puppy with another dog I strongly suggest that you walk him with his father, but get him away from his mother — don't let him see her again!' Anyway, she followed my advice and walked the pup sometimes on his own and sometimes with the sire and, from that time on, the puppy's suspiciousness quickly diminished and it showed no more fear.

The puppy progressed so well that it won show after show and very soon became an Australian Champion. Not only that, he went on winning and winning and when he reached the age of 8 years he won the veterans class at the Royal Melbourne Show where the judge commented so favourably by saying that she had never before seen such a fit dog with such a sound temperament at that age. Had that Chihuahua puppy not been taken away from his mother when he first came to me, he might well have remained suspicious for the rest of his life.

Another thing which can cause suspicion in puppies is where they are kennelled in a closed environment which has high solid walls or close-boarded fences through which they cannot see the outside world. They hear many strange noises, and because they cannot see what is going on they become very suspicious, bark in a frightened manner and run to the far side of their enclosure and possibly try to hide behind something like a small kennel. In order to prevent this cause of suspicion, breeders should always have their enclosures so constructed that the puppies can see what is going on around them. Some of the best guide dog establishments in the world, which breed their own stock, ensure that their puppy enclosures are made of cyclone fencing from the ground upwards and are situated at places where there is regular daily activity, so that puppies can see as well as hear all that goes on around them. It is essential that these puppies are fully conditioned to everything in life so that they can lead and care for their future owners who are blind.

Long-coated breeds of dogs can start to show suspicion in later puppyhood when hair grows over the eyes. Take for example the Old English Sheepdog. I have seen a number of cases where during early puppyhood these dogs have been quite all right. Then, when the hair starts to grow over their eyes, they start to bark at things, especially moving objects, because they cannot see well and do not understand what is going on. You cannot blame them really. I always liken it to trying to drive a car in the rain, especially at night-time, with the windscreen wipers out of action! You are unable to judge what lies ahead of you and the distorted glare of headlights from oncoming vehicles is terrifying to say the least.

Therefore, to prevent such suspicion developing in these cases, it is a good idea to carefully trim the hair in front of the dog's eyes or, in the case of show dogs, to keep the hair tied up in topknots, so that they can see quite clearly.

As I have said before, you have to try to understand how dogs see you in order to recognise their difficulties. With this knowledge you are then in a better position to help them.

Anxiety is a subject rarely referred to in dogs. I think the best way to describe anxiety is to say it is a state of nervousness. The usual cause of anxiety in dogs is where there is human stress and tension within the family in the home where the dog lives. And it appears that the more sensitive the dog is, the greater the chances of the person's anxieties being transmitted to the dog.

The reasons for human stress in this modern age are widely known. They include pressure at work, business problems, marital problems, financial difficulties, family discord, alcohol and drug abuse and so many others.

Of the many cases I have seen where dogs have been affected by the family's problems, one always stands out in my memory, mainly because there were so many problems.

A few years ago a man phoned me up to say that he had bought a German Shepherd dog, mainly as a guard for his house which he feared would be burgled. But the dog, which was kept in the backyard most of the time, barked all day, had become a nuisance and was most difficult to handle. He went on to say that he did not have time to handle and train the dog himself, but he would get his teenage son to do it.

I gained a fairly good idea of what the man was like by the way he spoke on the phone. He sounded very tense, full of his own importance, wanted everything done quickly and yet was not prepared to do the job himself. This impression was soon confirmed as he drove up to my house in his Jaguar car a few days later to keep his appointment. As he got out of this car I could tell by the expression on his face and the way in which he walked that he was a man under great stress and strain and that he was also a man who obviously had a lot of authority within his own company and was used to ordering people around him.

He got the dog out of the car and came over to me in a very pompous, business-like manner and said, 'Mr Tucker, the dog trainer?' 'Yes,' I replied quietly. 'Then here's my dog!' and he thrust the leash into my hand, as much as to say, 'You're the trainer, there's the dog, get on with the job!' As his 13-year-old son got out of the car he said, 'This is my son, and I want you to train him with the dog!'

Well, after the usual formalities I got on with training the dog and showing his son how to do it. As the lesson progressed I felt the boy did quite well, considering the dog was very strong and in great need of being calmed down. But what I found most annoying was the way his father kept chipping in and telling his son, 'Do what Mr Tucker tells you, right!' Throughout that first lesson he was continuously on to his son. It was nothing but, 'Do this! Do that!' and I got really tired of it, so much so that I had to tactfully steer his father away and ask him if he would mind walking several metres behind.

They came for their second lesson the following week, and once again his domineering father was continuously on to this poor boy who was trying his very best with the dog. So after a while I stopped them, took the leash and handed it to his father and asked him, 'How would you like to try your hand at training the dog yourself?' This took him completely by surprise. His face dropped and for the first time, he seemed stuck for words! After a while I said, 'Well, like your son, you have done quite well, although you probably did not find it as easy as you thought it was when you were telling your son what to do!' The point was obviously taken because he did not chip in again.

In subsequent lessons he did not bring his son again, but instead got the woman with whom he was living to drive his son and the dog over to my place for training. The woman also had a very naughty 6-year-old boy over whom she had little control, and he tried to tease the dog whenever he could.

I could tell that there were many problems within that household and during one lesson the son told me how difficult things were at home. While he tried to do his best with the dog, it was continually being teased by the 6-year-old boy. The domineering father was always too busy at work and never gave his son the love and help he deserved. They were always in fear of the house being burgled even though all the doors and windows were fitted with double locks and burglar alarms.

I never held out much hope for the dog living in such a tense atmosphere and after about five lessons they never came again. I often wondered what happened to the dog, but the moral of the story is that where there exists such friction in a home it does not give a dog much of a chance.

I well recall another case of how a dog was affected by a tense situation in the home. It concerned a guide dog which for some time had been working extremely well. Then things changed and the dog started behaving very strangely. It was then learnt that marital problems existed in the home. Finally, the wife walked out to live elsewhere, but from the time she left it was interesting to note that the guide dog settled down once again with her master. The episode was a very good example of how anxiety can show itself in a dog while it is living in a tense environment, but can quickly disappear once the cause of the problem is removed.

8 Aggression in Dogs

The thing that dog owners fear most of all is that one day their dog is likely to bite someone. Well, this does happen and always will from time to time. In most cases it has been caused and promoted by incorrect handling on the part of the owner. When this happens it is most unfortunate and regrettable. However, there are other causes for aggression which are beyond the owners' control and for which they should not be directly blamed.

First of all, aggression can be passed on hereditarily, and in cases where this does manifest itself, those who have bred the dogs should be held responsible. It is deplorable how some breeders will breed from a dog which may well have excellent show qualities, but at the same time has most undesirable aggressive tendencies. Good temperament should be regarded as of paramount importance when it comes to breeding.

There are four main types of aggression seen in dogs. They are *animal aggression*, *pure aggression*, *protective aggression* and *nervous aggression*. There are many ways in which they can start and develop. Most of them are caused in the early days of puppyhood by the owner holding the dog in close on a very short, tight leash. This frustrates the dog and because it is then linked so closely to the owner it takes on a protective role.

In addition to this, lack of socialisation with other animals can also promote aggression in the dog towards animals even though it may not be aggressive towards humans.

Pure aggression is where a dog is just purely aggressive towards all other people except its owner, and protective aggression is where the dog is protective over certain things such as its owner, home, car, kennel, food, in fact anything with which it is closely connected and regards as its own.

As I stated previously, mouthing should be stopped as soon as it starts, because it can often be a prelude to aggression. Also never hit your dog with anything, as that could make it aggressive and turn on you!

A male dog, when it gets to the age of about 7 months, will often try to have its own way, and unless you train it to obey and respect you, will soon have the upper hand. It might go to bite when you try to make it do something. This is where you have to be very firm. If you are weak and afraid of the dog, it will quickly sense this and have another go at you. The dog will try to be pack leader, but you have to show that it is not, but you are! It can be disastrous if that type of dog ever gets out and mixes with other dogs, becomes pack leader and then starts to chase and kill livestock.

Feeding a dog too many bones can make it protective. When you give your dog a bone I strongly advise that you do so indoors and not outside where it can bury the bone. If someone, especially a child, happens to stand near a spot where it buried a bone, the dog is likely to attack, thinking that the person is about to take its bone. You may not know the bone is buried there, but the dog does! Make no mistake about that.

Jealousy between two dogs over their owner can also lead to aggression. No matter how equally you try to divide your affection for both of them, or how you train and control them, jealousy is most difficult, if not virtually impossible, to cure. I always recommend that another home should be found for one of them. Fortunately, this trait is rare.

Always remember, never shout at a dog when you think it is going to have a fight, as shouting will only stir the dog up more. Instead, warn it in a positive, authoritative, calm, slow, quiet voice, 'No! Leave it!'

With aggressive male dogs of any breed I would always advise owners to definitely consider having their dogs castrated. The best time is around 9

months. If it is left much later, castration will cease more and more to have the desired effect. If left until the dog is, say, 18 months of age or over, there would be little point in having it done, because by that time the dog will have become really set in its ways.

I often see people who have little dogs pick them up when another dog approaches, and then wonder why their little dogs become so aggressive. The reason is that they are promoting protective aggression by holding their little dogs up against them.

A dog which has nervous aggression only shows aggression when and because it is frightened. So what you have to do, or at least try to do, is to keep the dog calm and boost up its confidence.

Last year a lady brought to me her Labrador-Border Collie cross, saying that she had recently taken it to her vet for the usual inoculations. Like many dogs, her dog did not really enjoy the visit, and because its toe nails were rather long she asked the vet if he would clip them back. This he attempted to do and the dog became aggressive towards him. He could see that his client had not much idea of controlling her dog, and that it had a temperamental problem. So he recommended that she should take the dog to me.

When she first arrived I could tell that the dog was timid and that it would not take much to upset her. Anyway, she continued to bring the dog to me every week for the next 6 weeks, and during that time they both picked up the training very well indeed. Also over that period the dog's confidence in me grew, and it showed much respect and affection. When she came the seventh time, I decided, half-way through the lesson, to let her relax on the lawn where I discreetly took each paw and clipped her claws! She did try to give me one half-hearted little nip, but I was that quick to give her a firm word, 'No!' and a jerk on the leash. After that I had no more trouble. Now obviously I was in a better position than her vet to do this as I was able to gradually get the dog's confidence, affection and respect over several weeks, but it does show that this type of aggression can be overcome.

I think it is worth mentioning here that there is a time when you are likely to see a bitch show protective aggression and that is of course when she has just had a litter of pups. This is to be expected and perfectly natural that she should protect her young ones. When the litter has gone she then returns to her normal self again.

From time to time such aggressive dogs are brought to me that I refuse to handle them. You have to see it to believe it. They are usually dogs which have been badly bred, mistreated, chained up, never taken out, teased by children poking sticks at them through the fences or who have had things thrown at them by the neighbours. My opinion, which is most often supported by that of the owner's veterinary surgeon, is that the wisest thing to do is to have the dog put down. Horrendous as the verdict may seem to the owner, I believe that we, as experts, are giving the right opinion. It is then up to the owner to look at the problem quite realistically and make that decision and take that step.

All we can do is to advise.

About once or twice a week people contact me to say that they have a dog which is potentially aggressive and that it is getting worse. By this time they have reached a point where they find that they cannot trust the dog any longer and that it has become a perfect worry to the whole family. What can they do? In nearly all the cases I refer to here, the owners have been lucky in having previously had dogs without problems. They have loved their dogs and given them a good upbringing, and then to get a dog which shows aggression really knocks the family. It makes them wonder what they have done to deserve this.

In strange cases like these it is necessary to get all the facts and this means asking the owners to try to recall every single thing they can think of from the time they purchased the puppy. In selecting one of these cases at random I hope I can give some guidance to people who are contemplating getting a puppy.

A lady who had brought her adult dog to me for basic obedience training 2 years ago phoned me recently to say that since she brought the dog to me she had had a baby who was now 16 months old. She was sorry to report that in recent months the dog had growled at a few people coming into their home, and more recently he had growled and snarled at their young baby which concerned them greatly. Then a few days ago the dog actually snarled at the lady when she was playing with him as he was lying on a bean bag.

We went right the way back over the dog's history and analysed all the facts. They bought this pedigree pup for a small amount of money when it was barely 6 weeks old. They actually felt at the time that it was possibly a bit too young to leave its mother, but were then informed by the breeder that the litter had been separated from its mother some time earlier. No reasons were given. I asked if they ever saw the sire or dam, and they said that they had not. This was a pity because I always believe that if you want to select a good puppy you need to be able to see the dam and sire. However, they did say that when they were selecting the puppy, another puppy in the same litter was so afraid that all it wanted to do was to hide itself behind the kennel, and would not come out at all.

However, they took home the pup which they had selected, but from the day they took him home he completely changed. Apparently he cried for months and months when he was put in his bed at night-time. This can be expected for two or three nights of course, but not for months on end.

Another thing they noticed about him was that he never played. He just did not know how to, there was no interest at all. But he did learn his obedience exercises as he grew up. Then when he was 5 months old he got out and received a knock from a vehicle and sustained a slight injury to his back. The veterinary surgeon who attended to the dog warned them that if any injury occurs affecting a dog's back it can affect the temperament, because as you know the spine is part of the central nervous system.

So it appeared that the injury had probably contributed to the dog's un-desirable temperament. Then a few months later they moved house and once again the dog found it very difficult indeed to settle into the new home. Soon after this they got another dog which had a very good temperament. Although he would grab hold of her at times and pull her around, he was very possessive over his bean bag and would prevent her from getting on to it.

Well, when I looked at all those factors, I could tell that the dog's mind was unbalanced and the great danger of course was that one day the dog would get worse and attack someone. You could liken it to a person in a mental institution who suddenly goes berserk — such a person would not be held responsible for his or her actions.

When you look at this case everything seems to be out of keeping. It is rare that a dog won't play and takes months to settle down into its new home. It was unfortunate that the pup and the rest of its litter mates were removed from their mother too soon. It was quite possible that the dam and/or the sire did not have desired temperaments. A dog which shows aggression to someone outside the family is bad enough, but when it shows aggression to the owner who has loved, cared for and trained it, that is completely out of keeping.

And so collectively there were a number of things which affected the dog's temperament. And I always say that in cases like this you must be realistic and very much aware of the potential dangers which exist. And so my advice was that it would be the best and kindest thing to have the dog painlessly destroyed before something went wrong which they may live to regret, particularly with their own child. The owners took my advice and although it was a difficult decision for them to make at the time it was a great relief to them afterwards.

In recent years I have been asked by members of the legal profession if I would examine, temperamentally assess and give evidence of opinion in court concerning allegedly dangerous dogs.

While I have been involved in this work, I have also seen the trauma that the dog owners have gone through and the distressing effects sustained by some of the victims the dogs had attacked. In two separate cases the victims were bitten on the face, one was where a 10-year-old girl was attacked by a Labrador and was so badly bitten on the face that she had to undergo a lot of plastic surgery over the course of 2 years. The dog was destroyed and the owners had to pay a huge sum in costs. In the other case a middle-aged lady was very badly bitten on the face by a Great Dane. Not only did she nearly lose an eye and had to receive much plastic surgery, but the terrifying incident of the attack affected her psychologically.

Another case was of a different nature where four German Shepherds molested a horse in a paddock, and a policeman had to fire a shot into the ground to frighten them off. The owner of the four dogs was charged with allowing her dogs to stray off her property, which resulted in them getting to this horse. I had the job of testing all four dogs. I found the mother was of excellent temperament and I could find no fault with her. But her three adult pups, just under 12 months, were quite the opposite. Two were very unsafe and the third was so dangerous I could not get near it!

After hearing my evidence and that of the local veterinary surgeon, which substantiated mine, the court ordered that the three dogs were to be destroyed. The owner was allowed to keep the mother, who was found not guilty.

Well, they are not very nice stories, are they? But when I quote those and others to people who are possibly heading for disaster like that, it really makes them think twice about continuing to keep their dangerous dogs. I hate to see people end up in court on those sorts of charges, and therefore will do all I can to prevent such problems ever reaching that stage by giving dog owners sound advice. It is then entirely up to them to take the necessary precautionary measures.

Unfortunately some people who own dangerous dogs will not take my advice to have their dogs put down, but want you to wave the magic wand, so to speak, and stop their dog from attacking.

A few years ago a man phoned me to say that he had a 3-year-old German Shepherd dog which he had had since it was 8 weeks old and that he thought it could do with some training. The way in which he spoke made me a little suspicious. I asked him, just as a matter of interest, why he had only just decided that his dog could do with some training, and did he have any problems with the dog. 'No!' he replied, 'I have no problems really. It's just that I thought he could do with some training!' He went on to say that his son, who was in his early twenties, would be the one who was actually going to train the dog. When they arrived a few days later, the son brought the dog up the drive to me while his father, who had got out of his car, watched from the other side of his vehicle in the road. This made me more suspicious!

I spoke to the son for some minutes, in which time I carefully observed the dog who was nosing around me. It was apparent to me that while he was a bold dog he was one to be handled with extreme caution. From the questions I asked the son and his replies, I strongly sensed that he had something to hide. Then finally it was disclosed that the dog had recently bitten his mother on the chest for no apparent reason. I had a feeling all the way along that something like this had happened. So I beckoned his father, who was about 15 metres (15 yards) away, to come up the drive to join us. I made this gesture discreetly and cautiously for I felt that if I signalled any more the dog might have attacked me.

He enquiringly pointed to himself as much as to say, 'Me?' to which I nodded my head, pointed to him and beckoned with my finger as much as to say, 'Yes, you, Sir! Please come here!' He did so with some reluctance and uneasiness. After having a short conversation with him, I said, 'I understand from your son that this dog has recently attacked your wife! I am very surprised that you did not tell me this when you spoke to me on the phone the other day.' He sheepishly admitted that that had actually happened, but for what reason he had

no idea. I then went on to say, 'Well, he seems to have settled down fairly well with me, so I'll now get on with showing you both how to teach him heelwork', whereupon the father said quite unexpectedly, 'I'm surprised he has taken to you. I would have thought by now that he would have ripped you to bits!' Well, I thought, if that is not an admission of his dog's aggressive temperament I don't know what is. I further asked him if he had had any experience with the German Shepherd breed, to which he said that while he was serving in the Royal Air Force overseas he associated with and used to watch the RAF police dog handlers give continuation training to their police dogs. However, I got on with the training for the next half hour and his son picked it up quite well. Then suddenly without warning the dog jumped up and grabbed me by the forearm! I quickly jerked him right up on the leash and held him there for a few seconds, during which time he let go and I lowered him down. Thankfully, he did not try that again during that lesson but there were no looks or remarks of concern from either the father or the son.

When they brought the dog the following week, the same thing happened. I had just completed a sit-stay on the leash with him, during which time he stayed perfectly still, and had returned to his right side when he jumped up and viciously grabbed me by the forearm. I effectively corrected him as I had done the week before. I then told the son to put the dog back in their car, which he did, and told him that I had made up my mind that I was not going to handle his dog again as it was so dangerous. For everybody's safety, especially his mother's, I strongly advised that the dog should be put down. His father sat in his car and made no effort to discuss the subject with me. I am still of the opinion that the dog had been taught attack work in the past and, as in most cases, it had got out of control.

Some weeks later I phoned them to ask what they had decided to do. The son, who was dominated by his father, was reluctant to talk to me, but did tell me that his mother was scared stiff of going near the dog, and that it was now chained up on the far side of their backyard where he could not get at her. I then spoke to his father, who told me that he had no intention of having the dog put down and that he would take the dog out for walks late at night when no one was around. Well, I could do no more, except to emphasise the point that to have a dog like that is like having a loaded gun — one day someone is likely to get severely hurt and it could be fatal.

About 2 years later I had a very similar case where a young man brought his dog up my drive while his father stood near his car parked in the road. By the manner in which the dog moved around and the sinister look he had in his eyes the whole situation was potentially dangerous. One wrong move and the dog would have attacked. To make matters worse, the slip-chain collar did not look strong enough and the leash looked as if it could snap at any moment. So I lent him mine for the time being. After a while I beckoned his father to join us, as I believed he could throw some light on to the dog's aggressive atti-

tude. I asked him if any member of the family had ever hit the dog, because by the way the dog was acting, I was certain that the aggressive tendencies it displayed had been caused by the dog being hit. Dogs cannot talk but they can show you a lot of how they have been treated. And the more experience you have in studying, handling and training dogs, the quicker and more accurate you become in reading a dog. Anyway, the father emphatically declared 'No! None of us has ever hit the dog!' I could also tell by the manner in which he spoke that there was an aggressive element in his nature.

By this time the son had put my slip chain and leash on his dog and had removed his own, which he then handed to his father. I was just explaining a few points before we set out for a walk, when suddenly the dog jumped up at the father. In a split second the man, with great speed, raised his hand so that the folded leash and chain collar flew back over his shoulder so as to bring it down on the dog's head to belt it! The dog instantly snarled with great aggression as I quickly said, 'Don't hit him!' I jerked the dog down and after he had settled I then turned to the father and said, 'You honestly say you've never hit your dog before?' 'Well, no, I haven't! That would have been the very first time I did it!' I quietly replied, 'I believe you have hit that dog many times, and I believe that for two reasons. Firstly, the way in which the dog has been behaving since he arrived here and the way he reacted by snarling at your face, and secondly, the way you instantly reacted. Anyone can tell that it has become a reflex action to you to hit the dog. True, your dog can't talk, but he can and has shown me how he has been treated!'

I decided at that point not to continue any further with his dog, the reason being that it was too dangerous. I was certainly not going to get chewed up for nothing and I would not have trusted the dog anywhere in the community. The aggression had been brought about by the cruel way in which he had been treated. I told the man this quite frankly and he more or less admitted it. I told him not to bring the dog back again and further advised him for his own sake and for the safety of others to have the dog destroyed.

Another very bad case of aggression that I experienced not so very long ago is one which I consider needs mentioning here. A 13-year-old boy, accompanied by his mother, brought his 6-months-old German Shepherd bitch to me for basic training. He was not particularly good with her and I felt that he could have done much better. I found her to be friendly and quite manageable. He came for three lessons and I saw him no more. About 4 months later his mother phoned to say that the dog was getting out of hand and that as her son had lost interest in coming any more, she had decided to train the dog. Every week she came, she complained that the dog was mouthing her. She showed me her hands and arms which were covered with teeth marks and scratches of claw marks. Week after week things seemed to be getting worse instead of better and then one day when this bitch was playing up, she flew at me and bit me

on the hand. I corrected her severely and went on training her and made her do as she was told. The moment she responded I gave her prolonged praise. All that time my hand was pouring with blood. I did not worry about that. What I was determined to do was to get the dog to obey and show her that I was not going to tolerate any aggression. Having finished on a good note I asked the lady to take her dog home while I drove to the local hospital for medical attention. There I received a total of eight stitches in my right hand.

The owner brought the dog along to training the next week as if nothing had happened. She never troubled to enquire about my hand, until I asked her how her son got on with the dog? She said, 'He gets on all right, even though he is not really interested in doing obedience training with her.' I sensed there was something strange about the whole case and felt that she was not telling me all that was going on at home. Two weeks later, I asked her what her son's reaction was when she told him that his dog had bitten me! She replied quite readily, 'Oh! He was highly amused!'. 'Highly amused?' I enquired, 'tell me, why?' 'Ah! Well, the dog had at last done what he has been teaching her to do —bite!' I stood there dumbstruck and puzzled for a while. I knew that she and her son were the only two living with the dog in their home; that he had supposedly given up training her in obedience, and that his mother had taken the task on, mainly because the dog was playing her up. So I asked, 'How has he been teaching her to bite?' 'Well, he wraps a thick towel around his arm and teases her up to attack it! He wants her to be like a police dog!'

I was naturally very angry when I learned of what had been going on over those past months. It was his dog, yet he was not interested in attending lessons in basic obedience. His mother, who went to work during the week, was being mauled nearly every day as she tried to train the dog in what spare time she had, while her son was teaching the dog to attack. I told her that, as his parent, she must take a very firm line with him and ensure that he never taught the dog to bite again. Furthermore, she was lucky in a way that the dog had bitten me and not another person. If it had bitten anyone else they would have had the right to sue her, which could have resulted in her having to pay high legal costs, etc., and of course the court would almost certainly have ordered that the dog be destroyed.

And that is why I do my utmost to persuade dog owners not to indulge in any forms of attack or guard work, because they may well live to regret it. I have had people who have either sent their dogs away to be trained as guard dogs or they have attended such classes with their dogs. I have witnessed such things going on. The trainers do not know what they are doing, brutal methods are often used and the owners are lured into believing that everything will be all right. Fortunately, some of the owners have enough foresight to understand the possible dangers that lie ahead and therefore pull out before it is too late and then sensibly join an obedience dog training club or seek private individual training from a professional.

On very rare occasions I hear of a dog which is continually attacking other animals, bites people and even turns on all the members of the family. Assuming that the dog has been well cared for, etc., the great chances are that the cause of such continual or spasmodic aggression lies internally in the dog's body. There could be something wrong either with the dog's brain or in other organs of the dog's body.

I know of quite a few such cases where dogs have appeared from the outside to be perfectly fit and normal, and yet it has not been until veterinarians have carried out exploratory operations on those dogs that the causes, or likely causes, for their aggressive behaviour have been revealed. To give a few examples — an enlarged spleen, an undissolvable stitch, and abnormalities such as an internal penis in a bitch.

Many years ago a guide dog which I had trained started showing aggression towards other dogs. It had been reared on the puppy scheme, carried out its training extremely well and was allocated to a blind man in the London area. About 6 weeks after he had been working with the dog he reported that his guide dog showed aggression towards other dogs in the street, but not towards people. We felt that this was absolutely out of keeping with this dog, having known it ever since it was born. The dog was brought back and I tested the dog by working it in the town and sure enough found it to be aggressive towards other dogs.

We then had the dog examined at the Royal Veterinary College. One of the leading veterinarians carried out an exploratory operation on the dog and found that when the dog had been spayed, a matter of a few weeks before she completed her training, an undissolvable stitch had unfortunately been left inside the dog, and this was irritating vital organs and was upsetting the dog temperamentally. The stitch was of course removed, and the dog was sewn up and quickly recovered. The dog underwent a little bit more training, and I am pleased to say that from that day on she never showed any more aggression towards other dogs. Conclusively, that was something internally affecting the dog and in that particular case the cause was an artificial thing, small as it was. I guess it could happen to anyone, working sometimes under extreme pressures, and a small mistake like that might occur only once in a thousand or more operations. It is nevertheless a very interesting case and although it was an unfortunate mistake, we were able to learn a lot about how a dog can be affected by some artificial body inside it.

Now I would like to tell you about a case in which a dog showed aggression quite unexpectedly and without apparent reason towards the owner's child. This German Shepherd dog was owned and trained by an instructor, who was a member of one of the dog training clubs in Melbourne. I personally knew the dog ever since she was about 8 weeks old and later saw her regularly when she was being trained in classes I was taking. She was a very fit dog. She had an excellent temperament and was brought up with children, all of whom she adored very much.

Then one day, when the dog was 13 months of age, while she was in the sittingroom with the family, she suddenly went for the owner's daughter and tried to bite her in the back of her head. If it had not been for the quick reaction of the father who instantly corrected the dog, the result could have been tragic. Because this aggressive act was absolutely out of keeping with this bitch, the owner immediately sought veterinary advice. One of the leading veterinarians who was particularly interested in cases of weight loss which are often associated with behavioural problems, examined the bitch and carried out tests for pancreatic insufficiency. Because these proved to be inconclusive, he opened up the dog to see what was wrong and found her spleen was very enlarged. He removed this and sewed her up again. She quickly recovered and was put on a special diet which consisted of only a little meat with plenty of vegetables. He also advised that all processed dog foods should be avoided as a safeguard against any possible disorder developing in the dog's digestive system. I am pleased to say that the dog continued to live a normal happy life and never showed any more aggression. So the quick-thinking owner who really knew his dog and the expertise of the veterinarian saved that dog from what could have become a serious problem, not only to its own health but also its approach to people.

Another strange case of aggression which baffled many people, including the owner and myself, concerned a female Dobermann Pinscher. The owner had the dog ever since it was about 2 months old, and it had an exceptionally good temperament when it was among people inside her home as well as outside. In fact, she adored everyone she met wherever she went, but she was very aggressive towards other dogs. The owner took her regularly to dog club to socialise her with other dogs and to train her in simple obedience. She performed all the heel-work very well, but was most unreliable in her stays, in which she would get up and dash around trying to pick a fight with any dog she could. Yet if the owner told her to stay anywhere else, where there were no dogs present, she would always stay. When travelling in the car she barked incessantly, especially when she saw other dogs passing, and was uncontrollable. Instructors did all they could to help the owner, but to no avail.

Then when the dog was nearly 3 years old, by which time the owner had just about had enough of her, the breeders offered to take her back, which was naturally very good of them. I think they felt it was the rightful thing to do realising that the owner had done everything humanly possible to cure the dog of its aggression towards other dogs.

Shortly after they had taken her back into their kennels, she came into season. So they tried mating her to see how she would react. Well, she reacted very aggressively towards the stud dog, so much so that the breeders strongly suspected that there was something physically wrong with her. So their veterinarian carried out a thorough examination followed by an exploratory operation to see if he could find anything wrong with the bitch.

When he opened her up he did not have to look far before he discovered that she had an internal penis. It was therefore concluded that it was the physical abnormality which was the cause of her aggressive behaviour, combined with the fact that some male hormones were probably being released into the system.

In the past 5 years I have seen two cases of uncontrollable aggression where dogs would attack (without fear) anyone, including their owners, when they came near. One was a Welsh Corgi, and the other a Chihuahua. Their brains must have been very badly affected for them to show such severe aggression. Nothing could be done and finally they were put to rest.

When I was instructing at the Royal Air Force Police Dog Training Centre, they received into the kennels some German Shepherds which had certain degrees of aggression. The vast majority of cases were the results of incorrect handling by their former owners. Realising they had to do something about the mistakes they had made, they took sensible steps by offering their dogs to the RAF in the hope that they could be successfully trained and put to good work in serving the country, and most of them did exactly that. However, there were from time to time cases of aggression which could not be cured or controlled, and as one of the Warrant Officers wisely and rightly said, 'When a dog shows aggression like that towards other people, including its own handler, then there is something wrong with its old brain box and the kindest thing for the dog and for the safety of all personnel concerned is to have the dog painlessly destroyed'.

I agreed entirely with him on this point, and to illustrate this I recall one such dog which had that problem. He was assigned to a very experienced and capable handler who managed to take him through the training course. But some time later, when he was on night patrol with the dog and completely alone in the middle of a huge airfield, the dog for no apparent reason and without any prior warning swung around and viciously attacked the Corporal. If it had not been for his expertise in being able to deal with that frightening and most dangerous incident, who knows, the consequences could have been much worse. The dog was duly destroyed by the vet. Not a very nice story, is it? But I quote it to show people what could happen to anyone at any time and in any place if they continue to keep that type of dog.

Those are just a few stories of the many I feel could be told. Abnormal behaviour caused by physical internal trouble in a dog is, I believe, an area which needs extensive research.

It is probably fair to say that in the vast majority of cases where dogs are suffering from acute or obvious pain, veterinarians would not necessarily believe that the medical problems which they diagnose would account for significant behavioural changes. This is of course understandable, because veterinarians usually see the dogs in their surgeries and only for a short time, unlike owners and trainers who are with the dogs for longer periods and observe them in a variety of con-

ditions. Furthermore, when veterinarians attend to dogs in their surgeries or elsewhere, the animals are often tense and extremely difficult to examine carefully. Sometimes those subtle problems can only be detected by surgery or blood tests. Apart from them being very expensive, they are likely to give results in only a low percentage of cases.

Naturally when vets have to examine dogs which are dangerous, they are very concerned about sending them home for further trial periods in case they bite again. Veterinarians will often comment on particular breeds and strains, and from their experiences the differences they see would indicate that there is definitely a genetic component which plays an important part in a dog's temperament and behaviour, e.g. strains of the Cocker Spaniel, especially the male golden-type, have shown a high incidence of aggression in the surgeries. I have seen evidence of this too, when dogs have come to me for training, or when I have visited the homes in which they live.

Among the multitude of things veterinarians have to deal with every day is the unpleasant task of advising clients that they consider, for the sake of all concerned, that it would be best for the dog to be painlessly destroyed. Upsetting as it is at the time, clients usually accept the death of an animal very quickly and upon reflection realise that this was the best advice. But all veterinarians should be made aware that there could be such a link between the various internal troubles dogs unfortunately sustain and the abnormal behaviour they develop. It is very easy to overlook or ignore physical ailments which can, in fact, affect a dog's behaviour, temperament and working ability.

Cases where a link has been established without doubt should be recorded so that a list could be built up of what could undoubtedly become a most interesting and valuable resource from which researchers could draw. It appears that up until now very little has been done in this particular area of veterinary science, but it is hoped that this area will be explored so that many of the mysteries expressed in abnormal canine behaviour can be solved.

It must always be remembered that when a dog is in shock it is highly likely to bite you, and bite hard. You cannot blame it. I well remember when I lived in England we had a very friendly Afghan, which I had known for 2 years, in the dog club. One evening it jumped rather awkwardly down off the stage in the village hall where we trained. It looked as if it had just ricked its paw and it lay there crying on the floor. I went over to look and it immediately grabbed hold of my foot. In order to get it off my foot I had to take hold of its jaws and as I did so it grabbed my right hand. The immediate pain was agonising. I then had to get my left hand into its mouth and pull its jaws sufficiently apart to release my hand. It all happened so quickly. As soon as it grabbed me, I knew that the poor dog was under shock, and as I stepped away I warned everyone to stand clear. Later it was carefully lassoed with two leashes and held between two handlers until the vet arrived to give it a shot

to put it out. He then took the injured dog back to his surgery and successfully operated on its front leg, which had broken when it fell. At the same time I was taken to hospital where I received a number of stitches in my right hand, which had been punctured in 16 places. Ah, well, I guess it is an occupational hazard, but wherever possible you should try to prevent or avoid such incidents.

In 1952 I attended a very interesting lecture given by a vet who told us how a dog followed his master to the railway station some kilometres south of London. The man boarded the train and as it pulled out the man expected, as usual, that his dog would return home. But this time the dog decided to pursue the train which accelerated at great speed. As the dog ran alongside the railway track he tragically touched the live rail. A signalman in a nearby signal box saw what happened and telephoned the station. Later, a porter with shovel in hand walked down the track to where the dog's body was lying. He dug a grave in the embankment and as he picked the dog up to bury him, the dog bit him and ran off up the track and home again! That is how a dog can be affected by an electric shock. He lay there supposedly dead until the porter attempted to move him. It was a lucky dog which lived to tell the tale, but another reason why I tell this story is to make dog owners more aware of their responsibilities, by ensuring that their dogs cannot get out and follow them to work or wherever they might go.

A little while ago now, I was exercising a Golden Retriever in a local park, when suddenly a Great Dane appeared from behind some trees and came towards him. Now it so happened that I knew that this particular Great Dane had an aggressive nature towards other dogs. The Retriever, which would do a brilliant recall, stood still as the Great Dane approached quite close. I knew that if I called the Retriever he would have obeyed, but I also knew that the Great Dane, who was only about 4 metres (13ft) from him, would have quickly pounced on him. So I considered it best to keep quite still and let them meet in their own time. The situation was extremely tense, but it would have been foolish to do anything which might have sparked off a fight. Then the owner of the Great Dane emerged from the trees on the far side, saw the two dogs sniffing each other, and said, 'It's OK, I'll just pull my Great Dane away'. I shouted to her, 'Please stay where you are. If you take hold of him or even go near him you'll without doubt promote a fight'. We kept quite still and waited patiently and after about 5 minutes the two dogs started to ignore each other and took to sniffing the ground. When they had about 20 metres between them, I said to the lady, 'Now very quietly call your dog and walk backwards, while I do the same with the Retriever'. This we did, and all was well. It was a tense situation while it lasted and it was best not to call the dogs until the tense meeting was over, and even then to do it very quietly.

This gives you a very broad idea of the different types of aggression and the many ways in which they can be caused and promoted. While a few of them can be cured, especially if they are caught in their early stages, others I regret to say cannot. Thankfully, wise and responsible dog owners take the most sensible step and have such dangerous dogs destroyed. Regrettably it is the irresponsible dog owners who decide to live with the problem. At least they admit that their dogs are dangerous, but it is very sad that they should have the constant worry that one day their dogs may cause grievous bodily and mental harm to people they attack.

9 Problems in the Home

It is really surprising the number of problems that people have with their dogs in the home! These problems are varied indeed. Some of them are very annoying, some are disturbing and some are most distasteful and quite unacceptable. While most owners try to do something about them, others just give up sooner or later and learn to live with them.

Most dog owners seek help from obedience dog clubs or dog trainers like myself after they have put up with their particular problems for some months. It is then a case of applying corrective training in conjunction with general basic obedience training. You may well ask, 'Can all these various problems be prevented in the first place?' Yes, I believe that they can, by nipping them in the bud as it were, as soon as they start.

One of the most common and frustrating problems people have with their pups or adult dogs when they first get them is urinating or making a mess on the carpet. The cause is simple to understand if you just have a look at the environment in which the pup was born. When it naturally relieved itself, who cleaned it up? That's right, the pup's mother! Of course she did, that is her way of keeping it and the rest of her litter clean. Later, when the pup grew and started walking around within the kennel enclosure, it relieved itself there. Then you bring the pup home, it sees your carpet which may be similar to the nest it has been in for, say, the first 7 to 8 weeks of its life, and it naturally thinks it is right to do it there!

What you have to do in order to prevent this from happening is to properly house-train the pup by regularly taking it outside to a special spot in the back garden and teach it to relieve itself there. When it does so, if you use a word like, 'Busy! Busy!', eventually it will obey on command at any time and in any place in which you happen to be. True, you are still likely to have the odd accident during the early days when it makes a mistake, that is to be expected. If this happens and you catch it in the act, just say 'No!' and take the pup outside to where it should do it. What you must not do is to hit the pup with your hand, whack it with a rolled-up newspaper or, worse still, rub its nose in it. Those sorts of acts are likely to make the dog worse and afraid, and it is then likely to relieve itself again out of sheer worry.

Another cause of puppies continuing to be dirty in the house is where they have been encouraged by their owners to relieve themselves on sheets of newspaper put down to cover a small area in one room. They have either read about this method in books or have received this advice from the breeder or their friends. They later become very dismayed when, having got rid of the newspaper, the puppy continues to relieve itself in the house. I always advise people not to use newspaper because, although they are teaching the puppy to go on the paper, they are also teaching it at the same time to do it in the house. So the answer is simple — don't use newspaper, confine your puppy to, say, two rooms, keep a constant eye on it and put it out regularly so that it learns the correct habit of relieving itself outside and in a designated area in your back garden. It is very much like teaching your child to use the potty! Do it regularly and praise the pup when it has performed.

Some people buy adult dogs and are most annoyed when they soon find out that they are not house-trained. Can this be cured? Yes, it can, but much depends on how old the dog is, how quickly it cottons on to what you want it to do and where and when. If it is a bad case of a male dog coming into your house and just lifting his leg on every bit of furniture he can, then I would first put him on the leash and slip-chain collar, take him to a tree,

tell him to 'Get busy!' Praise him as soon as he has done it. Take him a few metres away, then return to the same tree and repeat the process. You will generally find that he will do it again, even though the quantity of urine he passes is less. Repeat it once again. Usually three times is enough, but repeat it more times if you consider it necessary. At least you know that you have been fair in giving the dog the opportunity to relieve himself. Then take him indoors on the leash and watch him very carefully. As soon as you see him go to lift his leg on something or other, immediately say in a very firm, quick voice, 'No!' and give him a severe jerk on the leash. Now this corrective training may take a long time, but it is possible if you put your mind to it. Remember the golden rule: When you teach a dog to do something, or not to do something, always put it on a leash. The use of that, preceded by your command, is your means of control.

Incidentally, the same method can be applied to a dog which has been allowed to lift its leg on every street lamp post and gateway it comes to. Whenever I get a dog that has this habit, I show the owner how to get the dog to relieve itself a few times on one particular tree at the outset of a walk and, having done this, it should then be all right for about the next half hour. At the end of that time, I repeat the process by taking the dog to another tree and allowing it to relieve itself on my command.

I think it is fair to say that most people get their dogs to sit and stay while they put their food bowls on the floor and after a few seconds say,

Fig. 47. The dog is told to 'Sit' and 'Stay' while its food bowl is put down.

Fig. 48. The dog is told 'There you are, you can have it'.

'There you are, you can have it!' This is a very good procedure because you are getting the dog once again to respect you and obey your commands. But some people declare that although they have tried this they have not succeeded and have then completely given up trying. Really the task is quite simple. Have your dog sitting beside you with the leash held in your left hand. Tell it to 'Stay' and, holding the bowl of food in your right hand, slowly place it on the floor out in front of you and over to your right (**Fig. 47**). If the dog moves, say 'No!' and give it a corrective jerk on the leash, pick the food bowl up again, wait a few seconds and repeat the exercise. If done this way, dogs will soon learn to keep quite still until told they can eat (**Figs 48** and **49**). When you have gained this necessary control in a few days you can then do it off the leash.

Quite a number of people have difficulties grooming their dogs, which are always trying to mouth their hands or the grooming equipment. A lot of owners who have long-coated dogs often complain that their dogs do not like being groomed and become quite aggressive and turn around and bite them. Once again, it is all very simple when you know how to go about it the right way. Put the dog on the leash so that you have general control over it. When this is done, it cannot run off and you can give it the necessary corrective jerk if it starts mouthing you or the grooming equipment (**Fig. 50**).

Fig. 49. The dog is praised as it responds.

Fig. 50. If the dog is difficult to handle when being groomed, control it with the leash.

Now in fairness to any long-coated dog, whose coat can become so easily tangled, you need to groom it every day without fail. Otherwise if you pull against a knot in its coat with the comb, it will naturally hurt, just as if someone combed against a knot in your own hair. When a dog is hurt like this, is it not surprising that it would turn around quickly and bite you?

I have had a few clients who allowed small knots in their dogs' coats to remain there, even though they have groomed the rest of the dog. These knots get bigger and bigger until finally the only way to remove them is by cutting them off with a pair of round-nosed scissors. So groom your dog properly every day and it will enjoy and not resent the experience.

A very common problem which soon develops in a home where there are energetic young children living with a dog is when the dog runs after the children as they play and grabs hold of their legs. It is of course the chasing instinct coming out in the dog, and the children running stimulates the dog to chase and bite them. Consequently this upsets the children and if this trait is not corrected at the outset it will become a habit. Sheepdog breeds are renowned for this, especially when they are young.

I have had one personal experience of this when we had our first Border Collie in Australia. Our daughters were 6 and 4 years old at the time, and I soon learned that when I was not at home this bitch would tear after Sharon and Alison and grab hold of them by their ankles in play! Well, you can imagine how painful that can be because puppies' first teeth are needle sharp.

I then set about to cure the problem. Whenever I was at home I would ask the girls to run around, and as soon as Zena chased them I corrected her immediately by saying 'No!' and giving her a shake on the neck. Later, the word 'No!' given in a warning tone when I saw that she was just thinking about chasing them proved to be sufficient. However, further precautions had to be taken for when I could not be present, and so I explained to the children that it would be quite all right if they walked about in the back garden as long as they did not run. If they did wish to run around, especially if they had their friends in to play, then the dog was to be put inside the house. By everyone carrying out these procedures during Zena's puppyhood, the problem was soon checked and prevented from ever developing into a habit. Later, when she was a year old, and by which time she had had a fair amount of obedience training, she could be trusted to be in the garden alone with the children as they ran around and played, and she never chased after their ankles again!

Anyway, my advice to parents who have this problem with their dogs is to carry out this procedure and bear in mind that it is not just a case of training the dog, the children have to be trained as well; in fact, the whole family have to work as a team, especially in the first year of a dog's life, when the foundation of training for good behaviour is being laid.

From time to time you will hear of a dog which wants its own way and because the owner has not been firm enough with it in the first place, soon learns that it can have even more of its own way. The dog then expresses this by growling, which then leads to snapping, which can ultimately lead to giving the owner a severe bite. To give a few examples of this, some of the many problems I have been faced with, when people have brought their dogs for training, have included: jumping up on to a settee and refusing to get off when told to do so; picking up an object and refusing to give it up when the owner tried to take it away from the dog; refusing to go out of the house into the back garden; and many others. The list goes on and on. With all these problems just put the leash and collar on your dog so that you have that necessary control over it. Give it the one command like, 'Get off!' if you want it off the furniture, or 'Outside!' if you want it out of the house, and lead it in the required direction. If the dog dares to growl at you, say 'No!' and give it a firm corrective jerk without any hesitation. Show it that you are not going to tolerate any nonsense. What you say goes, and that is that! Do not forget to praise the dog as soon as it responds, and provided you are consistent you should soon overcome the problem.

The easiest way of dealing with these sorts of problems is to get on to them as soon as you see them start. Don't for goodness sake leave them, thinking that they will cure themselves. They won't. In fact, they are likely to get worse.

The same technique can be applied if a dog barks continuously or jumps at visitors, tries to steal food off the table, or scratches and whines unduly at the door. It can also be applied to a dog which is jealous of another dog in the house, and extreme jealousy can result in aggression. You have to assert that there is only one boss, one leader of the pack, and that is you, not the dog. However, you also need to closely examine the reason for it being jealous. You will need to ask yourself for instance if perhaps you have given more attention to one dog than you have to the other.

I have spoken at some length about the different types of aggression in the previous chapter, and while talking about problems which happen in the home I think it is appropriate to talk about protective aggression which can start and develop in the bedroom, of all places!

I always warn people wherever I possibly can to refrain from having their dogs sleeping with them in their bedrooms. This is bad, and even worse if the dog is sleeping with them on the bed. Because the dog is so close to them and they are lying flat, the dog can start to take on a more protective and possessive role, which leads to what is called protective aggression. This is promoted even more if and when the owner is ill. The dog will know this instinctively by its sense of smell and can become quite nasty whenever someone comes near the patient.

I have known of cases where, for example, the wife has gone to bed, then a few minutes later when her husband has attempted to get into the same bed, the dog which has been lying on the bed has challenged and

attacked him! And the same sort of thing has happened where the husband has got into bed first, and the dog has protected him by going for his wife when she had tried to get into bed. It sounds like there is a moral to this type of story, doesn't it? Perhaps it is how to get good grounds for divorce! Anyway, there are enough of those these days, we don't want more. So the obvious solution is, don't have the dog in the bedroom with you at night, and at no time when you or any member of your family is sick. It is just not worth running the risk. By all means have the dog in the house, but let it sleep in the laundry or kitchen or another suitable room.

Perhaps the most revolting problem is where the dog takes to eating its own motions. A number of theories have been given as to what causes this filthy act, ranging from the fact that the dog may be lacking in certain vitamins, to it being, as one English veterinarian once said in a lecture, nothing else but absolute vice!

Over the years I have seen it happen a number of times in exercise yards where there are many dogs kennelled. I honestly believe that in that sort of environment at any rate, the initial cause is boredom. After a while they get tired of playing with each other, and apart from the water bucket there is nothing else in the run except the motions which have been recently passed. The big trouble there is that it only needs one dog to start eating those droppings and other dogs are likely to copy. To prevent anything like that spreading, it is very important that kennel staff watch closely and correct the culprit immediately.

From then the dog should be run on its own, and its droppings be removed as soon as they are passed. Taking such precautions does at least minimise the spread of this filthy practice.

Personally, I have had only one dog which started it and this was at 8 months of age. So I put a few chunks of pineapple in her food every day for about 2 weeks and that cured her. The pineapple makes the dog's motions smell so putrid that the dog won't go near them. In fact, I noticed that she could not get away soon enough after she had defecated. This was not surprising as even I had to hold my breath while I shovelled them up to dispose of them each time. What we have to do, eh?

The last problem I wish to talk about which happens in the home is where a dog, for some reason or other, does not want to eat. This is somewhat rare, because nearly all dogs love their food, no matter what they are given. The reasons can be varied and quite baffling at times. Some of these dogs just don't like eating certain foods, in much the same way I suppose that some of us are rather choosy! Quite a few dogs won't eat fresh meat, but will if it is cooked. Some will eat tinned meat, but not fresh or cooked, and vice versa. Whatever the trouble is, one of the best methods to cure a finicky eater that I know of is to feed it in the company of another dog which is held on a leash or, if obedience trained, is told to 'Stay' about a metre away from the food bowl. In most cases the finicky eater will get stuck straight into that food, so that the other dog cannot have it! Continuous and enthusiastic praise should be given while it is eating and after it has finished. When you have used this method for a few days you should have no trouble and the dog will be quite content to eat on its own without the other dog being present. Keep giving the praise and hopefully it will start wagging its tail when eating, which will be a good indication that it is enjoying its meal. Great stuff!

10 Problems in the Backyard

It is not always realised by dog owners that a number of canine problems are caused by the type of environment in which dogs live. Sometimes conditions at the rear of their homes are extremely poor and the materials used in the enclosing surrounds are far from ideal.

It is amazing how some people move into a new home and, before they have adequate fencing and gates erected, decide to get a puppy. These people are just plain ignorant. They have no real sense of responsibility and they have not considered the puppy's safety and well-being. They expect their puppies to hang around their homes, and while some do at first, others walk off to become lost, get killed on the roads or are picked up by other people.

Those which do hang around the homes are quite likely to venture out every day, as they get a little older, and get up to all kinds of mischief from chasing cars to biting people (**Fig. 51**). It is not until this happens that their owners start to panic, grab the phone and contact the nearest dog trainer or dog training club for help. I receive a lot of calls of this nature

and have to tell these people quite simply and firmly that it is not their dog's fault, but theirs, and that they should have erected adequate fencing and gates before they thought about getting a puppy.

On the other hand, some people go to the other extreme and build high walls and close-boarded fences which, although the enclosed area is escape proof, do not allow the puppy to see through. Because the puppy cannot see what is going on on the outside, it hears many strange noises, starts to worry and becomes suspicious, and this is clearly indicated by the way it barks in a frightened way. Therefore you should have one section, say a gate at the side of the house, through which the dog can see people and traffic travelling along the road (**Fig. 52**).

It is unfortunate and difficult for people whose house stands on a corner, where children are able to tease the dog as they walk up the side street, banging on the fence or even poking sticks through it at the dog. Such cruel acts can soon make a dog not only suspicious towards people, but ag-

Fig. 51. Wherever possible the dog should be introduced to people such as the postman, so that it comes to like him and is not allowed to bite him.

Fig. 52. It is important that a dog should be able to see what is going on outside its property.

gressive as well. In situations like these it is necessary to construct a fence or brick wall over which and through which the dog cannot be disturbed or tormented by stupid and thoughtless young idiots.

I expect you have all heard of a dog which just runs around in circles all day chasing its tail! The usual reason of this is plain boredom, which is caused by the dog being left all alone in the backyard for hours on end every day. When a dog is bored it is likely to get up to all sorts of mischief, such as tipping things up, digging holes, pulling washing off the clothes line or barking excessively, which annoys the neighbours to say the least. Owners are ready to complain about all these naughty things their dog gets up to, but when asked if they ever take their dog out for a walk, they admit that they don't often saying that they never find the time. Personally, I always put the next question for their own self-examination and ask, 'Well, how would you like to be shut up in a small backyard all day and every day? Wouldn't it be enough to send you around the bend?' Feeling very guilty, they have to admit that it wouldn't be at all nice and then, with further advice, they realise that they must get their dog out regularly or find another home for the dog.

However, it is also possible that

91

there may be an unknown physical reason why the dog appears to be round the twist! I knew of a married couple who gave much time to their German Shepherd puppy. They socialised it well with other dogs and conditioned it to everything outside. It responded well to training and all in all was an adorable pet. Then one day, when it was about 6 months old, I noticed that it was having difficulties in the recall. For some reason unknown to us at the time, we could all tell that the dog was just not with it. It did not seem to comprehend. Its power of concentration was nil, yet it was not really distracted towards other things. During the next few weeks things became steadily worse, and then the dog became restless all day long. It was then put into another home, where there were two more German Shepherds, and it behaved just the same there. It would walk around a tree many times, then go to a bush and do the same. Because all this energy was being expended the dog became as thin as a rake. It acted as if the other dogs were not there. I took the dog out for a walk, during which time it took no notice of other dogs, people, birds, traffic, nothing! I tried giving it some simple obedience, but there was no response. I was quite convinced that there was something wrong with its brain. The next day arrangements were made to take the dog to the veterinary faculty at the university for further observation and diagnosis. After some days the report came back that the dog's brain was affected. Nothing could be done, and the dog was painlessly destroyed. Once again, I quote this type of story to show that some of the problems are beyond control and you just have to accept them.

This brings me to mention another problem which has similar results, namely loss of weight in the dog, but the cause is quite different. Occasionally a person brings me an energetic dog for training. While the dog has a very nice temperament and appears to be in good health, it is terribly thin. The owner explains that although the adult dog is fed twice a day and has been wormed regularly, it just does not seem to gain weight. I then ask if the dog does a lot of running around in the backyard and if it hurls itself at the fence as it leaps up to see what, if anything, is going on on the other side. Furthermore, is the yard enclosed by a high wall or close-boarded fence such that the dog cannot see unless it jumps up high. In most cases the owner admits that this is quite true. I then explain that a dog which is continuously jumping up like that is likely to lose weight rapidly, no matter how much it is given to eat every day.

I can recall a few cases when I worked with guide dogs where occasionally we would have a dog which would run from one side of the huge enclosed run to the other, jumping up at the high walls, even though the fourth side of the run was made of cyclone wire mesh from ground level upwards through which the dogs could see. The problem was easily cured by just putting the dog out into the run for limited periods, and the rest of the time when it was not working, it was kept in its kennel where it relaxed and could see the kennel staff at work.

Within a few days the dog started to put on weight.

An even worse problem of jumping is where the dog jumps fences! Once again, the most common cause of this problem is where the dog is not taken out for regular walks and is left on its own, sometimes all day, while its owners are out at work. The dog is naturally bored and also wants its owners' company, hence it takes to jumping the fence to get after them. When it has done this once that is the start of the dog becoming an escapologist!

Whatever the cause is, the best way of preventing a dog escaping is to add to the top of the fence a half metre (18in) incline at 45° facing inwards, made of strong strands of wire covered with wire netting — a security fence in effect. A dog would naturally fall backwards before it could climb over the fence, assuming of course that the fence is about 1.6 metres (5ft 3in) high.

I find that many owners who have this problem are people who have bought an adult dog from the lost dogs' home or animal shelter. Naturally they find this escaping most annoying, especially when they have never had this trouble with previous dogs for whom they have cared so well. It is therefore rightly assumed that the problem was caused and continued to occur when the dog lived with its former owner, with the result that the dog was eventually picked up by the dog catcher and placed in the pound and the owner never bothered to claim it.

Further to this problem is the well-known one where the dog follows the children to school! The children may or may not be to blame: the owner may have been negligent about keeping the gates and front door shut, or about ensuring that the gates had reliable catches. Some people have the complacent idea that because there is a fence, consisting of about five wires running through concrete posts, their dogs will not get out. But they soon learn that their dogs can get through if they really want to. Problems like these would not arise if dog owners used a little bit of plain common sense and ensured that they had adequate fencing in which to keep their pets and prevent them from straying.

To close on the subject of fences, I would like to mention the common problem people have when their dogs bark furiously, and often suspiciously, at neighbours whose heads appear over the top of fences! The trouble starts when a dog sees the unusual sight of a human head suddenly and unexpectedly appearing on top of a fence. To the dog it looks most odd and can prove to be very disturbing. Incidentally, this sight does not just appear on walls and fences. I have walked a dog down a street when all of a sudden it started barking at a man carrying a very large cardboard box out of a shop and straight towards us. All the dog could see was the box with a tiny head on the top walking on a couple of little feet! Another dog I took for a walk reacted in a similar way when she approached a technician who was repairing underground cables. From her eye level it looked as if the man's head was on the footpath! Several times I have carried a small high jump across a field where a few dogs, awaiting to line up in an obedience class, barked suspiciously because they had never seen a high jump move along on two human legs before! When I turned around and they could see my entire body they were quite happy and ceased barking.

So with all these things and the neighbour looking over your fence, you have got to tell the dog to be quiet, but at the same time take it up to the fence and reassure it that everything is all right.

Owners who have bitches in season should not think that because they have such adequate fencing to keep them in, they are safe from being accidentally mated. Although the female may not get out, a male dog could easily scale the fence and get in. Amazingly, the instinct for a male dog to mate is extremely strong. Dogs will stop at nothing to clear a very high fence to get to a bitch. In season time, then, if your bitch is normally in your house, it is best to supervise her running periodically in the backyard and then bring her indoors again.

If owners cannot be on the premises to cover the range of these particular problems, then I would always suggest that the dog be housed in a suitable kennel in a well-constructed and adequate-size run. Safe from the point of view of the dog trying to escape and safe to stop other dogs jumping in, as in the case of a bitch being in season.

Most people realise that all dogs need plenty of exercise, and some of them think that, because they have, say, half a hectare (1 acre) of ground for the dog to run around in, they do not need to take the dog out for a walk. This is quite wrong, in my opinion. All dogs should be taken out regularly, no matter how much property they live on. It is so important to keep a dog continuously socialised with people and other animals, so that it does not become frustrated, suspicious and, worst of all, aggressive.

11 Problems Outside

Taking a dog out for a walk every day should never be treated as a chore, but an enjoyment. It is all part of its education and for its well-being. It is so important to condition the dog to everything it is likely to meet, to socialise it with other dogs and other animals if possible, and to train it to be a well-behaved pet and totally acceptable in the community.

While many good, caring dog owners do take their dogs out every day, usually in safe, quiet parks where there are virtually no people or dogs, there are very few who take their dogs through a multitude of places of different environments. If more people did this, not only would their dogs be more reliable but I honestly believe that dogs would be regarded more highly than they are today. In this last decade or so there seems to be more and more restrictions on dogs. You may well ask: What can we, as dog owners, do about it? Well, I think there are several things. Firstly, and I have been saying this for some time now, what is really needed is a wide education program to make dog owners aware of their responsibilities and help them generally to know the best way to care for and train their pets. Secondly, dog owners have got to get their dogs out more and virtually sell the idea that dogs are good and necessary for humans. Thirdly, all governing bodies, whether they be canine or government, should update all their rules and regulations, many of which are unjust, ridiculous or outdated. Many of these regulations, which regretfully still exist today, were originally made in sheer ignorance by those who professed to know best.

I am always asking people if they ever walk their dogs through shopping districts, areas where there are other dogs, past schools when children are coming out, off their leashes in safe parks, or stand by a bus stop or just outside a railway station to watch people coming home in the evenings, and various other situations.

The usual reply I receive is that they try to avoid areas where there are other dogs, and shopping centres where they fear their dogs are going to shove their noses into shopping baskets. They avoid passing a school as children enter and leave, because their dogs may

Fig. 53. Shopping in the hardware store.

Fig. 54. Bank escort!

jump up at the children, and they avoid parks at certain times because their dogs may chase and jump all over the joggers.

Now all that avoidance is a great pity because they are not giving their dogs that further education they need, and what is more they are not getting the general public used to seeing good dogs being properly and responsibly trained. This, I believe, is so necessary to promote good dog ownership in society today.

When I secured my present German Shepherd at the age of 7 weeks, within 3 days I took her to the shopping centre and carried her in my arms into the bank where both staff and the few customers who were there fell in love with her, like most peope do whenever they meet a puppy, regardless of breed. I did the same in the local post office and hardware store (**Fig. 53**).

I kept this up regularly, but after a while, at the rate she was growing, I found her too heavy to carry, but by this time she was quite happy to walk in on the leash and sit against the counter. Well, as you can imagine the local community got used to meeting her as she grew and grew, so much so that if I happen to go into the bank without her, the tellers and manager inquire, 'Where's Jade today'? (**Fig. 54**).

I also made a point of taking her to the local schools two or three times a week for her to see the children coming out. Naturally a few of the children wished to stroke her, which I welcomed very much, and it was not long before the word got around among the children and I had quite a lot of them wanting to meet her as they hurried home. Some months later when I had taught her the stand for

Fig. 55. Standing her at the school crossing.

Fig. 56. Introducing her to the petrol pump attendant at the service station.

examination I would stand her at the kerb of the school crossing and have the lollypop lady run her hands over her. Later some of the boys and girls did the same when they came out of school (**Fig. 55**).

Whenever I pulled into a petrol station for petrol I took the step of taking her out of the car immediately and introduced her to the petrol pump attendant, and then let her watch while the tank was filled up. You see so many dogs in the backs of cars go crazy when suddenly a strange figure quickly approaches the back window and makes a bit of noise as the petrol pump nozzle is inserted into the tank. But by letting my dog watch all this from outside the car and then taking her into the office to pay for the petrol, she accepted it so well and built up a good association of ideas whenever I visited a petrol station (**Fig. 56**).

As time went on I took her to many different places in order to condition her to every situation possible. These included the busiest streets of the city of Melbourne and among the bustling

crowds at the Victoria Market (**Fig. 57**).

In her early days of puppyhood when I let her off the leash for a free run in a safe park, which was far away from traffic, she kept within a few metres of me. But as she grew she became more confident and ventured further away to investigate things. This is always a good sign to see and it is fascinating to watch how a puppy changes and gains more confidence in itself. Then one day at the age of 5 months she saw a jogger and decided to run after and play with him! Unfortunately, he started waving his arms about saying, 'Get the dog off me! Get it off! Get it off!' His arm actions only made her more excited and she thought it was great fun! Eventually, I managed to calm the man down and asked him to stand still while I put her leash on to give her the appropriate correction. She tried it again the next day with someone else and although she responded to my correction I felt that it was likely to happen again. So I decided to nip this one

97

Fig. 57. In the market.

in the bud before it developed. I took her on a longish leash up to the same park between 5.30 and 6.00 pm for that was the time when the greatest number of joggers would come through the main gate into the park. As each one came in we walked towards him or her and when she gave the first indication of wanting to run, I said 'No!' and gave her a jerk. After giving a few corrections like that I was able to warn her with just the word 'No!' without a jerk. She soon responded and later I was able to do it off the leash. Two days later I did not even have to say 'No!', but as the joggers approached she would look over her shoulder at me, as much as to say, 'Are you still watching me?' And that was precisely the impression I wanted her to have, and one which I like to see exist between all my clients and their dogs, 'Yes, I am always watching!'

When people come to me with their dogs for training, once I see that they have fair control of their dogs I then take them to such places as shopping areas, past schools, through parks and so on. They can then apply their training under all those conditions, especially if they are having difficulties, like their dogs being distracted in those particular areas. Sometimes of course they have learnt all their basic obedience at a dog club, and while they may work well in quiet conditions where there are no distractions, they will not work where there are distractions. So I tell them that that is exactly where they are going to work! The owners often become apprehensive, and sometimes even give a gasp of surprise. 'Nothing to worry about,' I assure them, 'after all that is what you've come here for. You want to overcome this problem of your dog being distracted, so we will go to an area where there are plenty of stray dogs, and there you can practise as much as you like and get your dog to obey and pay attention to you. It is no good evading the issue, we have got to do something about it, and now's the time.'

We arrive at an area which I have nicknamed 'Dog Alley' and put the dog through an intensive session of heelwork, sometimes making the dog go past a barking dog several times until it does so without even looking at the distraction. It does not take long for the dog we are training to get the message, and at the same time the owner for the first time realises that he or she has to be very firm, and go at it again and again with full determination. The dog gives in and gives greater respect to its owner, for which it is praised and the owner comes away with a great sense of achievement. From that point on there is usually no looking back.

I always say in my lectures, or when I am training people with their dogs, that training demands an attitude of firmness and determination. Whenever I am handed a dog to train my attitude is one whereby I say to myself, 'I am going to train this dog! It doesn't matter how long it takes or what various methods I might have to use, but I will train it. If the dog has a strong will, mine will be greater'. The dogs I refer to are, of course, those which are not suffering from any fear or those which are dangerously aggressive.

This is the attitude I like my clients to have; I never like to hear them say, 'Oh, I'll never be able to do that', or 'I'm sure my dog won't do it!' In fact, I quickly tell them that I never want them to have a negative attitude, but a positive one and for them to say, 'Great, I've seen you do it, I'm now going to do it myself!'

There are some dogs which will heel

Fig. 58. Walking a dog at heel in a shopping area.

quite well and do good sit-stays, but when it comes to doing these exercises in shopping areas, disobey repeatedly. There are two main causes for this. Firstly, the dog is naturally distracted towards pedestrians, and secondly, the owner has been reluctant to correct the dog in front of other people. The dog soon finds out what it can get away with and continues to disobey. So to correct the problem you have to work on the dog! It is quite simple really. All you have to do is to select a stretch of footpath outside a row of shops and carry out strict heelwork, correcting the dog immediately and wherever necessary, and praising it on every response it makes (Fig. 58). Then do a sit-stay outside a shop, like a milk

Fig. 59. Doing a sit-stay outside a shop so that the dog learns to stay quite still.

the conversations, the dogs get up, turn around, pull on their leashes, sniff the ground and even the people passing by. Eventually, if they have good memories, the owners realise that the last command that they had given their dogs was to sit and stay. They had not told them to go free. Is it any wonder then, if dogs are allowed to get away with this, that they will do it at any time and in any place? Well, there it is, always remember to be consistent and remember what the last command was that you gave to your dog.

Taking your dog to a shopping area should not be for the sole purpose of doing obedience, it should be used mainly for getting the dog used to the variety of conditions which are to be found in those places. When people bring me puppies which are around 3 months of age, I like to spend one lesson taking them to the shops, mainly to teach them how to introduce their puppies to everything, especially if they happen to be their first puppies. Some of the pups are highly excited, of course, and therefore it is a good idea for owners to park their cars a little way away from the shops and, having got their pups out, to stand for a little while to allow them to get used to their new surroundings. Then they can walk in a quiet relaxed way towards the shops. This stretch of walk allows pups time in which to settle down so that they are much more manageable by the time they reach the shops.

One of the things dog owners find hard to do is to talk to their dogs. Most will feel very self-conscious about saying all sorts of things to their puppies in front of other people in the

bar, where there will be a steady flow of individuals going to and fro across the footpath from their cars to the shop as well as pedestrians walking up and down the footpath. Once again every fault is corrected and in a very short time the dog will learn that it has got to stay quite still while you are out in front of it holding the leash **(Fig. 59)**.

As with all exercises, you must be consistent at all times. You will often see owners sit their dogs on the footpath while they talk to people. During street. They imagine that pedestrians will think they are silly talking to their dogs which cannot talk back! On the contrary, they don't, and when I point out that their pups need their support and that the main means of support is in the correct use of their voices, owners start to realise and appreciate that they must do this for the benefit of their puppies if they want them to enjoy their walks and not feel afraid of anything which they may encounter en route.

So, taking the puppy, I show the owner what to do. As we approach a person I say to the puppy in a very interested and enthusiastic tone, 'Who is that, then? Do you want to say hello? There's a good dog — you can meet him then!' While I am saying this, I make sure that the stranger can hear what I am saying and my eyes glance rapidly from puppy to person to whom I smile. Apart from giving this support to the puppy, the person can quickly and readily understand what I am trying to do and because I am saying such words he or she assumes that the puppy or dog must be quite all right, otherwise I would not be saying such things or allowing it to walk along on the full length of a loose leash. I then follow this up by saying, 'Good morning! How are you?' And it is surprising how many people will stop as I go on to explain that we are just getting the puppy used to people so that it is friendly to everyone it meets in the future. As people bend down to the puppy, I ask them to let the puppy sniff their hands and then stroke the puppy slowly underneath its chin and down its chest, because that is where the pup likes it

best. By using those words it is pleasing to see how many people will cooperate with my requests. During the time the puppy is getting acquainted with people, I tell them the dog's name and continue to talk to it, saying something like, 'There's a good girl Sheba! Who is this then? There's a clever girl. That's right, you say hello! There's a lovely little girl'.

Very often people will go on to ask more about the puppy and then like to say a few words about some of the dogs they have owned in the past. It is very good when people do this, because once the introduction has been made it is quite possible you will meet the same person or persons some days later when you are out with your puppy. And so the more introductions and handling your puppy receives, the better. As we depart, I always thank the people for giving their time and for stroking the puppy we are walking. They naturally appreciate this and feel that they have contributed in some small way in getting the puppy accepted into the community.

When approaching children I use another phrase like, 'Look, Sheba! Here come the children! Would you like to say hello to the boys and girls?'. The children then understand that I am talking to the puppy about them (**Fig. 60**). I find children are very good when introducing a puppy to them and I always start off the conversation by asking them if they like dogs and if they have dogs at home. This makes them feel good when they know someone is interested in their dogs or dogs they have owned, and some of the conversations I have had with young children have been very interesting and quite amusing.

Sometimes you don't have to make any real effort in introducing a puppy and this is when the child wants to meet it first. Whenever a child says, 'Oh, Mummy, there's a doggy!', I always ask the mother if her child would like to meet and stroke the dog, to which she nearly always replies, 'May he, please? He loves dogs'. This, once again, is an opportunity not to be missed.

In Australia, and in other countries I believe, there are many people who unfortunately still have a fear of German Shepherds. However, people's attitudes to the breed are far better now than they were, say, 20 years ago, but there is a long way to go yet in convincing people that it is not a vicious breed, as some have been mis-led to believe. Therefore I urge those people who buy German Shepherds to make every effort in getting them out into the public when they are puppies and keep it up. This is the only way, as I see it, that people are going to accept it as a trustworthy and first rate working dog, provided it is bred well and is properly socialised, conditioned and trained.

Now in contrast to this correct procedure of introducing a puppy to the public, just imagine how tense and unsure the puppy would be and what would happen if the owner held it on a short, tight leash and never said a word to it. Even if the owner did say something like, 'No, leave them alone!' as they walked towards and past people, those pedestrians are likely to think that the owner has a vicious or potentially dangerous dog

Fig. 60. Introducing a puppy to children.

just by hearing those few words which have been said to the dog. Unfortunately most owners don't realise that if they hold their dogs on short tight leashes they are in great danger of promoting any potential protective aggression. So remember to keep the leash slack and assure the public with what you say that it is a good dog.

Lastly, I would like to say a few words about getting puppies used to the sight, noise and movement of traffic. It is always best to walk your puppy on a quietish road first and each time a car comes along, stop and let the puppy watch. Talk to it quietly and stroke it gently to give that reassurance it needs. Keep the leash slack so that if the puppy wants to move away, it can. Don't hold it in tight, as it is likely to panic if it gets even the slightest of frights.

When you reach a main road, don't

Fig. 61. A puppy can be conditioned to the sound and sight of traffic.

take the puppy right up to the kerb, but stand a few metres back. From this position and angle it can see the vehicles coming gradually from both directions and each will appear to be at its level (**Fig. 61**). If you took the puppy right up to the kerb, every vehicle would appear to be coming faster, louder and towering up above it. This could terrify a puppy. So remember, approach traffic carefully, so that the puppy gradually gets used to it and builds up confidence in itself.

It is another simple case of preventing problems of fear before they ever start.

I believe that giving dog owners this tuition for when they take their dogs on the street is an essential part of the entire training program of handler and dog, and I would like to see dog training clubs cover this aspect far more than they do. After all we should first and foremost be educating our dogs to work well and to be totally acceptable in the community.

12 Problems in the Car

There are quite a number of problems that people have with their dogs in their cars. These can range from dogs suffering from car sickness and a general dislike for the car, to dogs which are quite uncontrollable, even to the point of showing protective aggression to people who come anywhere near their cars. With most of these problems it is best to take steps to prevent them ever starting rather than having to cure them with corrective methods of training.

Perhaps the most baffling problem is car sickness. It is not really known what causes it, and probably there are a few reasons. But you can carry out a variety of preventive procedures in the hope that your dogs will not develop car sickness. I think the first thing to do is to get a puppy into a stationary car so that it becomes well acquainted with it. To do this you need to talk to the puppy a lot so that it enjoys being in the car. The next thing is to take it for a short trip in the car. Just around the block will do for the first time. Avoid doing this just after the puppy has had a meal and make sure the car is well venti-lated. Choose a cool day, as a hot or even warm car can distress a puppy. If you see any signs of car sickness, stop and get the puppy out for a while. As the days and weeks go by, try gradually extending the distance and time the puppy is travelling in the car.

A lot of people ask, 'Where is the best place in a car for the puppy or adult dog to travel?' Personally I like to have mine on the floor in front of the front passenger seat. In the early days, the pup can be secured there by a short chain attached to the underneath of the seat. This is an ideal position in which to have a puppy, as you can quickly glance down and reach over with your left hand to correct it if and when necessary. The puppy also feels secure because it is fairly close to you and is more likely to respect you because you are in a commanding position (**Fig. 62**). Another reason why I choose this place is one of safety. If I ever have to brake suddenly the dog would just lean against the place where the passenger's feet would rest. This is all right if you have a dog no larger than, say, a fully-grown German Shepherd. If you decide to have

Fig. 62. When travelling with a dog in a car you need to be in a commanding position.

something like a St Bernard, then it might be best if you get yourself a suitable van. One of my clients, who had a St Bernard, had a bright idea with his Austin Mini. He removed the front passenger seat and replaced it with a wooden floor on which his dog, weighing 90 kilograms (200lb), could stretch out in the down position the full length of the interior. This worked extremely well.

But, it might not always be convenient to have the dog in the front and therefore it would have to travel in the back. This is safe if the dog is behind secure bars or a grill, but if the dog was on a seat and you had to suddenly brake, the dog could be thrown forward either around your neck or through the windscreen! One of my friends took the precaution of this happening and tethered her dog by means of a harness and very short leash secured to the back seat. A very sensible idea. Always ensure that windows are lowered enough for the dog to breath the fresh air, but not too low so that it can put its head out of the car. Apart from the possibility of the dog developing eye trouble caused by constant wind or any foreign bodies such as flies and grit, allowing a dog to have its head completely out of the window can and does promote excitability, barking and trying to snap at vehicles as they pass. This is one of the causes of dogs becoming uncontrollable in the car.

When people bring dogs to me for the sole purpose of curing their bad behaviour in the car, which by this time has possibly been going on for many months, I tell them that they must get the dog to obey the basics in obedience before they have a chance of curing the problem in the car. What you want from the dog is *respect*.

Having taught it basic heelwork and the sit-stay, I then apply this in a very practical way by telling the dog to sit and stay while the car door is opened, and it is not to move until told to get in (**Figs 63** and **64**). The same sort of procedure is applied when getting the

Fig. 63. The dog is told to 'Sit' and 'Stay' while the car door is opened.

Fig. 64. As soon as the dog enters the car and sits on command, it is praised.

dog out of the car (**Figs 65** and **66**). I then go for a short drive around a quiet block and if the dog misbehaves I stop and it gets the necessary correction — either a jerk on the leash or a shake on the neck. If the dog is very bad, I then get it quickly out of the car, march it up and down the footpath, putting in some very quick sits and about-turns. This is the quickest way of getting the dog's respect again. Then it is put in the car again and I drive on. Concentrated training like this has the desired effect. The dog very soon realises that if it misbehaves it will be corrected immediately, whereas in the past it has barked and barked and got away with it as the owner has had to continue to drive through busy traffic and virtually had no control over the dog. Possibly the only thing the owner has done during

those times is to shout at the dog in the car in trying to tell it to be quiet. But shouting is about the worst thing you can do in such a small, confined area of a car, and only stirs the dog up even more. What you need to do is to speak very firmly but as quietly as possible and give the dog a physical correction.

Dogs which are allowed to bark in cars while travelling, often start doing it when they are left in cars and, if they are not corrected immediately, will continue to develop the habit. This can lead to protective aggression.

I have met quite a few dog owners who have foolishly encouraged their dogs to bark in cars, thinking that by barking they will deter people from stealing the car. I tell them that I train my own dog to sit quite quietly in my car. Even when she is in a huge super-

Fig. 65. The dog is told to stay as the car door is opened.

Fig. 66. The dog is then called out to sit at heel while the door is being closed.

market carpark where there are many people walking by, she must not bark. The very sight of her sitting there alert, is a deterrent to any would-be car thief. And that, I think, is what you should aim for.

You always hear of dogs and children being left in closed cars on hot days and the results have proved to be fatal. This is nothing but absolute ignorance, negligence and lack of consideration on the part of those who have left them in those suffocating conditions, and I think it would be very remiss of me if I did not make mention of these horrifying accounts, of which you hear every summer. It must be realised that a closed car can reach extremely high temperatures in a matter of minutes, and therefore every precaution must be taken to see that humans and animals are not in

any way subjected to such dangerous conditions.

There are some dogs which are very reluctant about getting into the car and some which won't get in at all. There are different reasons for this. It might well be that the owner has forced the dog into the car instead of encouraging it and making it a pleasure for the dog. It may be that the car was too hot. It may be that when it went in last time, it was then taken to the veterinarian to have an inoculation which it might not have liked very much. The dog associates the car with going to the veterinarian, and therefore takes a dislike to the car.

Whatever the cause, you have to do all you can to encourage the dog in and try to establish a good association of ideas in its mind. The method I use, which has not failed yet, is to have the car in the drive with both back doors open. With the dog on the leash I get in first and call the dog up on to the back seat, make a fuss of it and go out the opposite door, calling the dog after me. Then I get the owner to do this a few times and the dog thinks it is great fun and its confidence grows.

Now a few words of advice about getting a puppy into and out of a car. Always lift it up completely and gently place it. Neither expect a pup to jump up into a car, which will be a strain on its back legs, nor expect it to jump out of a car, which will be harmful to its front legs as it lands on the ground. Remember, take care of those little limbs as they grow and develop. Also ensure that the puppy is right in and that its tail and ears don't get caught in the door when you shut it!

I would say that in a very short time every dog owner who takes his or her dog regularly in the car to a variety of places, whether those trips are frequent or infrequent, soon notices that the dog gets fairly excited when they are getting near to a place it knows. Owners can readily understand this, especially if they are travelling short distances of, say, 15 or 30 kilometres (10 or 20 miles) in daylight hours. But they are puzzled to know how a dog, which has been fast asleep for a long time as they have driven a long distance of, say, 150 kilometres in darkness, knows when it is within about a half a kilometre from home! Well, the answer is simple actually. Every district has its own particular smell, and although the dog is fast asleep its sense of smell is still at work. Even if you have all the car windows up, the smell of the area will get into the car through the vents and fine cracks. This will stimulate the dog's phenomenal scenting powers and it will get up and indicate that it knows you are nearly home.

So even when your dog is fast asleep, it does not matter where it is or where it is travelling to, its sense of smell is working like a computer! Isn't it wonderful!

13 Problems in the Show Ring

The problems which constantly occur with show dogs of any breed are numerous indeed. Some dogs have poor temperament, most have not received the basic training that they should have had, many have faults which are the result of incorrect handling and quite a few dogs have been frightened by, I regret to say, some of the judges!

With dogs which suffer from poor temperament, you can usually blame either the breeder, who has bred from undesirable stock, or the owner, who has not conditioned and socialised the puppy properly in the early months of puppyhood.

To breed for a good temperament should be of paramount importance. It matters not for what purpose the dog is being bred, whether it is for showing, breeding, obedience trials or working dogs of any kind or just a family pet. It is very sad and most annoying when breeders breed from particular stock which may have excellent conformation, but does not have a good temperament.

However, the majority of cases of poor temperament, and I am mainly referring here to dogs which are suspicious of people and other dogs, are because the dogs have not been conditioned and socialised properly by their owners in taking them out regularly to different places which have a variety of conditions.

It is quite a well known fact that the lives of some show dogs consist of living in their kennel environment, and travelling in the car every week to dog shows, and that is about all these dogs see. What a restricted life for a dog! Some dogs are not even allowed in the home, yet when you visit the home trophies galore adorn the mantelpiece and every other available piece of furniture, and the walls are covered with so many dog show ribbons, sashes and certificates that wallpaper is not really necessary! I expressed this view once during a public meeting, and unknown to me there was a gentleman in the audience whom I was to visit some kilometres away later that week in order to give another lecture to a large group of handlers, followed by a practical dog training session. The point I made must have pricked his conscience, because I learned later that when he returned home that night he said to his wife, 'With what I have heard Michael Tucker say tonight, we'll have to get most of these ribbons down off the walls and get the dogs out of the kennels and into the lounge before he gets here in 2 days time!'

Now while people can show their pups as young as 3 months of age, it does not mean to say that all pups are ready for this. You should consider each puppy as an individual and if you do not think that it is ready for the show ring, then keep it out until it is ready. If you push a dog too early, you are likely to upset it and that will ruin it for good and you would live to regret it. It is much better to be patient, act sensibly and wait. I also direct this advice to people who wish to enter for obedience trials or any other working trials of that nature. Most of the actual problems with the dog in the show ring are caused by incorrect handling and not training the dog to walk properly on a loose leash.

When people come to me for training in show work, I insist that they learn how to walk a dog on a loose leash, so that the dog is happy, relaxed and attentive to the handler. I feel very sorry for those dogs which are hoisted up on tight leashes as they are paraded around the ring. I am very pleased, however, to see the occasional judge penalise anyone who has a tight leash. If every judge did this, this fashion of tight leashes would soon cease. I have seen some dogs held so tight that they could hardly breath and have been seen to stagger. And as you all know, quite a few handlers hold their dogs

up on tight leashes in order to hide certain faults their dogs have!

Perhaps the most common problem of which you will hear exhibitors complain is the fact that his or her dog is generally badly behaved in the ring. It pulls, jumps up, twists around, barks, sniffs the ground, will not stand still, grabs the lead in its mouth and is very distracted towards other dogs. Collectively, all these faults point to one thing — lack of respect! It is as clean-cut as that. All that is needed is basic heelwork: to walk straight and close without pulling, to do the turns neatly and to obey the command 'Stand', and to stay quite still, especially when being examined by the judge. Many show people are very adamant that you cannot mix obedience with show work. They are of course quite wrong. In fact obedience complements show work, and show work complements obedience. A large number of people, who have brought dogs to me with good conformation, have explained that they just cannot seem to win or even get places. But after they have learned how to give their dogs basic training, they have then gone back to show work to win time and time again, and it has been a pleasure to watch them work in the ring with their dogs on loose leashes and obeying the commands.

Having taught your dog to walk at heel on a loose leash, the next thing to do is to get your dog to stand immediately you command 'Stand', and to stand perfectly straight beside you. This is quite simple. All you have to do is to take hold of the leash near the clip in your right hand, give a firm command 'Stand' and immediately give the dog a backward jerk along its right shoulder, simultaneously locking the dog's left hindleg back with your left hand, which is cupped and lands on the front of its stifle. If you do this quickly you will get an instant response. You will also notice that your left forearm will be touching the side of its body and this will keep the dog straight and prevent it developing the habit of bowing out to the left. The instant that the dog halts, let go of the clip part of the leash with your right hand, and bring your left hand around to slowly and gently stroke the dog's head as you praise it vocally. By using this quiet, slow manner you will keep your dog calm, and it is less likely that it will move. After a few days of consistent training it will soon stop on command only, without you having to apply your hands to your dog. The next stage is to do all this when gaiting the dog. But a word of advice here, have your hands ready to immediately uphold your command, because when dogs are trotting along they are not so quick to stop as when they are walking at a normal speed.

Having taught the dog to stop instantly, the next thing to do is to place its feet correctly. Place the front feet first, straight and at the required distance apart, depending on the breed of dog, then adjust the hind feet in a similar way. When you place your dog's hind feet, for instance, pick each paw up gently by the hock and place it accurately where it should be. Avoid pushing the dog's foot along the ground, which will only rub its pads on the ground surface, and this is not nice for the dog if the ground is rough.

Fig. 67. Standing a dog at the edge of a step or down kerb.

So remember, gently lift and place accurately with the least amount of handling. While you do this have hold of the leash, short and in the other hand, so if the dog moves you are in an excellent position to correct it with your voice and an appropriate jerk on the leash. The next thing to do is to command the dog to 'Stay' while you step around in front of it, and eventually you will be able to encircle it. Many dogs during their early training are always likely to move and, whenever this happens, they should always be taken back to their original places and made to stay again. To emphasise this point, it is quite a good idea to stand the dog at a down-kerb so that its front feet are on the edge or a few centimetres behind the edge (**Fig. 67**).

111

To move forward the dog would have to step down on to the road. If it tries this you must immediately correct it. What is interesting to see is that it has a greater meaning to the dog to stay quite still if this is taught at a kerb edge, or any step, rather than anywhere else on flat ground. Later, when the dog really obeys the stay, you will be able to get it to do so anywhere.

Well, that is all quite straightforward when you are dealing with a bold type of dog which is just a bit of a fidget! But now look at the dog which moves out of the way because it is suspicious of the person who wishes to physically examine it. Every dog has some suspicion. That is only natural. What you have to do is to help your puppies and dogs get over their suspicions by supporting them with a reassuring voice as you introduce them to people and the many things they will encounter in life.

One of the things that must be prevented at all times is to stop puppies and dogs seeking security by trying to hide behind you when you approach someone, or someone approaches you. If this is allowed to happen, then it will become a habit to the dog, and the longer it continues the more difficult it will be to cure.

It is very similar to a small child who is shy and actually hides behind his mother when she meets someone out on the street. Quite often such a mother will admit, 'My child is very shy, you know'. Such a remark can have an adverse effect on the child who will become worse. The right thing would be for her to teach her child to say, 'Hello!' to the person they meet. When you use a parallel in human relationships, you become aware of your responsibilities with your dog. You must run your hand down the leash to control and prevent the dog from getting behind you and, at the same time, use encouraging words like, 'Good dog, go and meet him, say hello, there's a good dog!' A young dog will soon learn that you will not allow it to hide behind you and that if it goes up to the person it will be praised.

When you have a dog which shows some suspicion towards people, always ask them to remain where they are and take the dog up to them. This approach helps to boost the dog's confidence. In contrast to this, if a person approached you and your dog, he or she would have a threatening effect on the dog. I direct this advice partiulcularly to instructors in obedience dog clubs when they examine dogs. After all, they are there to instruct people how to train their dogs.

Sometimes it takes weeks and months to overcome suspicion and I always tell people not to worry if their dogs move around a little while they are being handled by someone else, as long as they don't get behind you. It is very important that the dog is allowed to relax. This would not be so if the dog was a bit suspicious and you insisted that it stand stock-still. When, and not until, the dog has reached a stage whereby it is happy, relaxed and confident about being handled, you can command it to stay in the stand position and be handled by someone while you remain at its side. A dog gains a lot of confidence if it can rest its chin in one hand of the examiner while he or she runs the

Fig. 68. A dog gains a lot of confidence if it can rest its chin in one hand of the person who is examining it while it is stroked with the other hand.

other hand over different parts of the dog's body (Fig. 68). If the dog seems quite happy about all this you can then say 'Stay', and leave your dog by turning around and stepping out just in front of it. Only remain there for a little while and return by the same way to your dog's side, and after a few seconds gently and quietly praise the dog. As the weeks go by, you can approach the person who is going to examine your dog, and halt a metre

or so away so that the person will only have to make a very short approach to your dog. As the dog continues to build up confidence, the person's distance of approach can be gradually and carefully extended.

In all these gradual stages both the handler and examiner should talk quietly to the dog. Some years ago I covered this subject in great detail when I delivered a lecture on handling. I later learned that there was a man in the audience who had just started judging in the show ring and was particularly interested in what I had to say. About 2 years later I happened to show a young dog under this judge and to my great delight he talked to every dog as he carefully and gently examined all the dogs in every class. The result was that he carried out his job without any hassles. All the dogs were happy and relaxed and so were the handlers.

In contrast to that I have, as I am sure you have, seen some very heavy handling on dogs by some judges. Fortunately they are in the minority, but I honestly wonder at times how they ever obtained their judge's licence! Nevertheless it is something you must be very much aware of, because one bad move on a judge's part when examining a puppy can ruin its showing chances in the future and this can be heartbreaking for the owner.

Quite a common fault seen in the show ring is where handlers cannot walk or run in a triangle. They seem to run in any shape but a triangle! As you all know, three straight lines make a triangle. If this is not done, not only can it annoy the judge, who wants to see, from where he or she stands, the dog from directly behind, from the side and from the front, but it can concern and spoil the dog if the handler runs into it.

In training therefore, it is best to run in a large triangle and as you start aim at a particular reference point and keep glancing up at that point as you gait the dog in that direction. Turn left when you get there and aim at the next reference point. Turn left when you reach there and aim at the last reference point. Now this you have to imagine is the judge, but as you proceed along this third side of the triangle aim just a little to the judge's left side so that your dog, which is on your left, will be in line with the judge. The same sort of thing applies when you are required to run your dog away in a straight line, left-about turn and return in a straight line and stand the dog in front of the judge.

If you have difficulties with this, try running your dog along and return on a straight white line like you would find on a soccer pitch or tennis court. This makes you very conscious about your footwork and when you can run straight you are not likely to cause gaiting problems with your dog.

A funny little problem you sometimes see is where a dog stands on command and then holds up one front paw! This usually happens with some of the small breeds when they are being set up on the table in the ring. You will then see handlers trying to pull the raised front leg down, but to no avail — it just goes up again and again! Now it is very easy to correct this fault. All you have to do is to take hold of the other front leg and attempt to lift it up. You will then see the dog

Fig. 69. Give your dog a daily mouth examination.

put down the raised leg. Repeat this corrective technique as and when necessary and you will soon have your dog standing on all four legs!

Lastly, comes the part of the dog the judges always want to see, namely the mouth and teeth. Quite a few dogs rebel against having their mouths examined, not only by their owners but by veterinarians and show judges. Well, the simple answer to this problem is that you, as owner, should examine your dog's mouth every day, and from an early age, so that it is used to it. Get the dog to associate the examination with pleasure by stroking it gently first, talking to it all the time and then gently lifting one side of the top lip up, then the other **(Fig. 69)**. Do this quite casually; don't make an issue out of it. Later you can start opening its mouth, and don't forget plenty of praise. If by any chance the dog does try to bite you, make sure you have it on the leash whereby you can give it a corrective jerk. Then make another gentle attempt at looking at its teeth and praise it as it behaves. This is all quite easy if you go about it the right way.

I could tell you of many amusing stories connected with showing dogs, and one that always comes to mind was when a lady phoned me to ask if I could help her with a problem she had with both her Weimeraners in the show ring. Apparently they used to go to sleep standing up! Anyway she drove just over 150 kilometres to see me with these two dogs. They were lovely dogs, well behaved and gaited beautifully in perfect triangles. They stood on command and she held the leash up tight and above their heads. Within a few seconds their eyes would close and remain shut, just as she had told me. So next time she stood each dog I asked her to lower her hand so that the leash and slip chain collar was loose. Hey! Presto! The dogs' eyes opened and remained open. The problem was cured. I explained that the way she was holding the leash up tight was restricting the dogs' air flow and they started to get drowsy! Well, there it was. She went home happy, feeling that it was well worth the long trip. One can be lucky sometimes when problems like these can be fixed in a matter of minutes, but most take much longer.

14 Your Vocal Control

It does not matter for what type of work you are going to train your dog, your main means of control is the correct use of your voice.

Learning the words of command or short phrases is quite easy, although many people do say the wrong words in their early days of training, but to use them with the correct intonation is harder and needs a lot of practice. In other words, it is not exactly what you say to the dog, it is how you say it that really counts.

In making the right intonation you have to express yourself in so many different ways, depending on the nature of the dog and the circumstances at the time.

Most faults in dog training are allowed to occur because the handler has either had a monotone-type voice which is useless or has not used the voice at all with the result that the dog continues to have its own way. You really have to put feeling into it. When you praise your dog, smile and say 'Good dog!' as if you are so very pleased with it. If it is excitable and needs to be quietened down, say in a calm, slow, quiet voice, 'Steady'.

When it needs to be corrected, frown and say in an abrupt, quick, firm tone, 'No!' If it is ever unsure and starts to lag behind, use an encouraging tone with an exciting flavour to it and say, 'Heel, lad, there's a good dog, clever boy!' When you carry out a right, or right-about turn, where the dog has a greater distance to cover than you when you turn around, say, in a very interesting voice and raise your eyebrows in glee, 'Bobbie, heel! Good boy!' What you are really conveying to the dog in those few words is, 'Look Bobbie, I'm going this way now, come with me'.

On some occasions, where you anticipate that the dog is going to do something wrong like chasing after the local cat, put a warning tone in your voice, 'No! Leave it alone!' as much as to say, 'I know exactly what wicked thoughts and intentions you have! Well, don't you dare even think about them, because I am the boss and I'm watching you! I'm always watching you'. This is a very good example of prevention, which is much better than saying nothing, allowing the dog to lunge at the cat and then having to give it a correction after the event.

All your specific words of command should be said positively, although they should have slight variations. For instance, the command 'Sit!' should be said quickly and sharply, as the air is expelled from your lungs through the gap in your teeth, if that is the best way to explain it. This should get a quick response from the dog. The command, 'Stand', can be said positively but in a higher note and more drawn out, and the command, 'Down!' or 'Drop!', should be given in a very deep tone. When it comes to commanding the dog to 'Stay!' in any of these three positions, this should also be said in a very positive way, as if you really mean it.

Unfortunately a lot of people are not positive enough, and this can be clearly seen and heard in the way they give their commands. Instead of telling the dog, they tend to ask it, 'Sit?', 'Stand?', 'Down?', 'Drop?' and 'Stay?' with the result that the dog rarely obeys but instead just walks away to do just as it likes.

There are times when you do need to use an excitable tone in your voice and this is when you are teaching the dog to fetch something, go over jumps and various obstacles, or even to quicken up a recall.

When you get into more advanced stages of training you may have to use an enquiring tone in your voice. This is in tracking or any exercise to do with scent work where you are dependent upon the dog taking you to the person it is tracking or finding articles. In such cases you are asking the dog to use its initiative and natural ability to find. If trained properly, this

is where the dog really helps you, but you still need to play your part even though you are dependent upon it.

Well, I expect you can think of other tones you use when you talk to your dog throughout the day. Sometime try jotting down all the words and phrases you use in a day. It is simply amazing how long your dog's vocabulary is.

The difficulties which handlers have in using their voices are quite numerous, and if these are not overcome then problems with their dogs are bound to arise. Many people are embarrassed about using their voices in public, when really they have no need to be. In fact the general public admire people who talk quite freely in controlling, encouraging and praising their dogs.

I learned this time and time again when training guide dogs, particularly when my colleagues and I were training in the busy city of Melbourne. People would often say, as they stood beside us waiting for the traffic lights to change, or as we worked through huge department stores, 'How nice it is to hear you trainers talking to your dogs, you can obviously see how and why the dogs work so well because of it. It seems a great pity that more people don't talk to their dogs in this way.' What they heard was very true and their kind remarks were greatly appreciated.

Another fault is where people use their voices far too loudly and this tends to either disturb or excite their dogs. Nearly everyone knows that a dog, provided it is not deaf, can hear far better than any human being. So why shout? I believe the only time you should shout at a dog is when it is a long way away and that is only to make your voice carry, especially if the wind is coming towards you.

I shall always remember one man who came to me with a few problems with his German Shepherd. He had been attending a dog training club for nearly a year. So I watched them do about 2 minutes heelwork on the leash just to see how they worked together before I tackled the problems. Well, I have never heard such a loud voice from a man as he bent down and yelled down the dog's ear the commands 'Heel! Sit! Stand! Stay', etc. I walked over to him and quietly enquired, 'Tell me, is your dog deaf?'. With a somewhat puzzled look on his face he said, 'No'. 'Well, then why is it,' I asked, 'that you shout at your dog?' 'Oh! That's simple,' he replied, 'if I did not shout at him he would not obey me! The instructors at the dog club have told me that'. 'Well, I'm sure the dog will obey if you use a quiet voice!' I assured him. 'Would you like me to work him for a few minutes?' 'Please do!' he welcomed, and handed me the leash. Well, I more or less whispered to his dog all the commands to which he obeyed so willingly and gave me greater attention than he had ever given his owner. When I handed the dog back to him, he was flabbergasted and then said, 'I would never have thought my dog could ever work so well, and what is more you are a perfect stranger to him.' I felt that here was a case where one could not blame the owner, but the instructors in the dog club for telling him to shout the commands. Well, from that day on he kept the volume of his voice right down and what problems he did have, most of which were caused by him shouting at his dog, I soon ironed out.

The speed at which commands and short phrases are given is another important factor in vocal control. For instance, when walking a dog freely on the leash and the dog suddenly starts to surge forward, you need to say, 'Steady!' very slowly and quietly, give the dog a quick, firm jerk on the leash, relax it and upon response say in a slow, quiet, calm voice, 'Good dog'. You should also walk slowly in the circumstances because this also helps to keep the dog calm. Walking quickly will tend to excite the dog. In contrast to that if you said, 'Steady!' and 'Good dog!' in a quick voice you are likely to excite the dog and it will surge forward again. The point to remember here is that you have got to do all you can to calm the dog down.

I'll always remember one funny incident when I showed a lady, whose dog was most excitable, how to use a slow, quiet voice to calm him down. She exclaimed, 'Oh! I could never speak like that to my dog, my friends would think I am retarded.' So I just said, 'Don't worry about what your friends will think, just think of your dog! He is the one you are training! I have to talk to dogs every day in a variety of ways, including a lot of quiet, slow talking, and no one has yet thought I'm retarded!' Anyway, I'm glad to say she soon came to understand the point I was making and followed my advice.

Giving other commands slowly like 'Sit!' for example, will either result in the dog sitting slowly and possibly in a crooked fashion, or not at all. Such words should therefore be given quickly in order to get a quick and instant response.

How then are handlers going to know how to use their voices? Well, as I see it, the answer is very simple — instructors have to teach people how to speak to their dogs, and this is a thing which is sadly lacking these days. Instructors have to therefore have an imaginary dog at their side to whom they talk so that the handlers they are instructing can copy what they say and how they say it. It does not matter if they are teaching one individual with his or her dog or a large class. When instructing, instructors should briefly explain the exercise, and when saying the appropriate word or words of command, should put the intonation into those words and explain why they should be said that way. They should then follow it up by giving a brief demonstration with a dog, once again emphasising the intonation for the handlers to use. Finally, when they practise, instructors should insert those words of command into their general instructions so that the handlers can copy the intonation. So in the case of teaching heelwork they should say, 'Are you all ready? Forward, HEEL! GOOD DOG! Now you are all doing very well. Keep walking straight; keep your eyes on your dog; say "GOOD DOG!" Now we'll get ready for a halt, prepare by getting your hands and leash in the right position, get ready, handlers, halt, SIT! GOOD DOG!'.

If instructors keep this up until the handlers know exactly what to do, what to say and how to say it, they will eventually only have to say 'Forward' and 'Halt' and the handlers will do the rest themselves. The interesting thing about all this is that the handlers will eventually have voices just like the instructors! Lucky people!

As I have said before, a lot of people are not positive with their voices. One command in particular which I have found that they do not say firmly enough is 'Stay!'. Even when I have said, 'Stay!', they say to the dog 'Stay?'. I repeat it again and ask the handlers to *tell* the dog and not *ask* it. Often their second attempt is much better and I will say, 'That's much better. Now say it once again very firmly as if you really mean it, STAY!'. This time they say it really well and as soon as they say it like that I say, 'Excellent! Leave your dog!'. One feels a little bit like Professor Higgins in Bernard Shaw's 'Pygmalion' and its musical adaptation, 'My Fair Lady', when he painstakingly teaches Eliza Doolittle to speak properly! It is very much like learning the proper pronunciation of foreign words when you are attending a language class.

Another fault which can create many problems is where the reflexes of handlers are too slow when they are correcting their dogs vocally. With appropriate training, which I have covered in Chapter 2, handlers can learn how to quicken their reflexes and to improve their powers of concentration.

Yet another fault in training which can lead to many problems is where people do not praise their dogs at the right time. Perhaps the best example of this is seen where people call their dogs and they never praise them until they arrive at their feet. They should of course praise as soon as the dog makes the first response to come, that means as soon as it takes the first step towards the handler, no matter how far away it is. Once again it is very simple to get a handler to praise the dog on the response. I do this by placing a piece of cord or a spare leash on the ground and in front of the dog, about 1 to 1.5 metres (3 to 5ft) from where a dog has been told to stay, and instruct the handler, who may be about 10 metres away, to call the dog and praise it before it crosses over the cord or leash. This method certainly makes a handler very much aware of when he or she should praise a dog, not only in the recall exercise, but in any exercise.

Correct timing in using your voice, your signals, your actions and positions when training is of great importance and becomes a real art. Can this be taught? Yes, I believe it can. And in saying this I hope it will give people confidence and an added incentive to strive with determination to achieve success. Naturally it needs a lot of concentration and practice and it is to be expected that different people will reach varying levels of success.

Many people have great difficulty in recalling their dogs in areas where there are distractions even though their dogs understand what the recall exercise is all about. This then becomes a major problem. Each dog may come to start with, then lose interest, run off to play with a child or dog, sniff around trees or along the ground, run past or run rings around the handler, or even run to the handler's car so that it does not have to do any more recalls

or training. Whatever it does it won't come. One of the causes, apart from lack of respect, is that the handler has not said the right word at the right time. Now with this type of dog and this type of problem you must remember first of all that there are three basic things to say:

- the recall command, 'Come!';
- the words of praise, 'Good dog!';
- the corrective words, 'No!' and/or 'Leave!'.

What it amounts to is that as soon as the handler calls the dog, 'Prince, come!', he or she must praise the dog on its initial response and keep that praise flowing until the dog arrives at his or her feet. But if the dog diverts in any other direction, which of course is wrong, the handler must immediately and firmly give the corrective word 'No!', followed immediately by the word 'Come!'. The dog must then be rewarded with praise the instant it responds. These three things, while they will be said quite rapidly, must carry the appropriate intonations, namely 'No!' should be said with a tone of displeasure (not frustration), 'Come!' should be said in a firm tone and 'Good dog!' should be said in a very pleasing manner.

While some people can apply this with the instructor standing nearby prompting them, others get mixed up with the words, use the wrong intonation and find it difficult to give the commands at the right time.

Now when I see a case like this, I don't like to see the dog get away with it, or be confused by the incorrect timing of the handler's words. Also I don't like to see a handler get himself or herself into a state of frustration because the dog won't come or, worse still, give up and turn around and say, 'Well, I told you what would happen — it does this every day to me'.

So before we do it again with the dog, I take the part of the dog and tell the handler that he or she can practise on me as long as is necessary. I instruct him or her to think of and say the three things as and when they are needed, and in return I will abide by the rules of the game until I decide to run off again, just as a naughty dog would do! Just before we start I remind the handler that I will come the moment he or she calls me, but if I do not receive immediate praise, I will stop in my tracks; and if I run off in another direction it will be no good just saying, 'No! No! No!', I must be told what he or she wants, which is 'Come!'. followed by the praise as I respond.

So the game starts. The handler calls me and I respond, but because there is no praise given as I take my first stride, I stand still! There is silence for a moment and it then dawns on the handler why I have stopped. He or she then gives the praise which I acknowledge by saying, 'Thank you very much!' and run towards him or her. Then all of a sudden I take off in an-

other direction. After a few seconds the person says, 'No!' and keeps repeating it. I continue to run around and say, 'Yes, you have said "No!" but what else do you want me to do?' There is a pause again and then he or she says 'Come', which I do. I go about two steps, and because there is no praise forthcoming I stand still again. He or she then realises why I have stopped, and then gives the praise to which I respond. And so the game goes on and on until the person gets the perfect timing of the words and really it is the naughtiness of the dog I am portraying which makes the handler quicker and accurate. At the same time the handler does not get frustrated. On the contrary, we always have a good laugh about it afterwards. When the handler has mastered this with practice, which does not take long, I then ask him or her to do it with the dog. And what a difference! The results are great. The handler gains so much more confidence and control while the dog soon realises that when it obeys it will be immediately encouraged and rewarded with sincere vocal praise, but if it disobeys it will receive an instant vocal correction.

Where there is a will, there is a way, and dog training can be great fun as well as a challenge.

15 Your Physical Control

When people take up dog training they very soon find out that they have to learn far more than their dogs. This is quite true and it always pleases me when clients realise and admit this, usually half-way through their first lesson. As a matter of fact I always welcome them saying this rather than me telling them, because it shows they have the right sort of attitude towards training. In contrast to this, people who blame their dogs for everything, or who are not prepared to put time and effort into training, or expect a trainer to do everything, have the wrong attitude altogether and therefore will never succeed. Fortunately and thankfully these people are in the minority.

However, even though nearly all the handlers have a good attitude, many of them have difficulties in walking straight, co-ordinating their hands and feet, making full use of their body weight and being flexible enough in using their bodies correctly as they learn how to train their dogs. You have only to watch good labourers for a while to see how effectively they can use a pick or shovel, or athletes excel themselves on the sports field to realise how much the human body can do and endure if it is used properly. Training dogs all day is no exception to this and I have always believed that if we go about it the easy and proper way we will get the maximum results with the minimum amount of effort.

Owning a dog certainly provides you with a purpose for going out for daily walks and, as you know, walking is one of the best forms of exercise you can have. But when people take up training their dogs it is surprising to see how many handlers cannot walk in a straight line, and a fault like this can adversely affect their dogs, especially highly-sensitive dogs, by making them walk wide while heeling. They then become wary of the handler's feet. Why can't people walk straight? Well, there are a few reasons for this.

Generally, unless people have been in the services where they have received a lot of training in marching and other forms of drill, or have perhaps done calisthenics, dancing or anything similar when they were young, they have never really had to concentrate on walking straight. A lot of people are grossly overweight and this can affect their balance; quite a few are very tense when training and tend to wobble over, while others may unfortunately have various physical disabilities.

Now for the good news! Can these difficulties be overcome? Yes, in most cases they can. All it requires to make handlers very conscious about walking straight is determination from them and the necessary assistance and advice from their instructors.

Learning to walk straight should be emphasised right from the outset of training, and I advocate to all instructors who take classes that they should get handlers to walk abreast of each other and *not* to follow each other around in a circle. That certainly does not teach people to walk straight. On the contrary, it teaches them to walk into their dogs when they walk around in an anti-clockwise direction, and this in turn makes dogs heel wide which is not what is wanted.

There are various ways of getting people to walk straight. The one I favour first when training an individual, is to face the handler and walk backwards, and ask the handler to aim straight at me when heeling his or her dog. Then, when coming to a halt, to keep their toes pointing towards me as they sit their dogs. After they have done this for a little while, I move away and ask the individual handlers to imagine that I am still walking backwards in front of them. They do this and achieve success.

When they work alone in their local areas I advise them to aim at a reference point, like a tree or fence post,

Fig. 70. *Right turn*
Having walked along the white line, turn right at the corner by pivoting on the right foot first and bring the left foot beside it, giving the dog about half a second to respond, then proceed along the next white line.

as they start off and to keep glancing up at it. As soon as they do a turn they should aim for a new reference point. Another way they can help themselves is to walk along white lines in a car park or on a tennis or basketball court. These lines are ideal because they can also perform their right-angled turns with great accuracy (**Fig. 70**).

All these methods make people very conscious about walking straight, so much so that eventually they are able to walk straight and turn accurately without the aid of reference points. People who are tense have first to try to relax and then use the methods I have just mentioned. For those who are overweight, then I think they know the answer to that! Yes, lose weight! But I know it is not always easy for them to do so, even though they would like to. However, I would always advise them to stop and put their right foot out to the right when they come to a halt. This gives them a much better balance. This also applies to people who have very large, heavy dogs which tend to lean against and push them over!

A great number of dog owners eventually admit that the problem they have is that their dogs have become too strong for them to handle. This is very true where the owner is below average height and weight and not physically strong enough to control a huge, strong dog whose weight is often more than the owner's. In cases like these, it is best for another person in the family, who is strong enough and has the height, body weight and control, to train the dog. But in other cases where owners do have the required physique to handle large, strong, heavy dogs, even though they don't think they can, they are surprised by what they can do when they are shown how.

First of all, it is a case of teaching handlers how and where to grip the leash correctly, how to jerk the dog effectively and to relax the leash immediately. Also, how to make full use of their body weight, and how to place their feet. Regular training teaches them to be more alert, their reflexes become quicker and they learn to develop the art of reading their dog's intentions. Collectively, when these

Fig. 71. To correct pulling in heelwork, take hold of the clip part of the leash with thumb on the top, command 'Heel', jerk back *horizontally*, then let go and stand still.

techniques have been learned, handlers soon find they have the overall control they need.

The most common problem in heelwork is a pulling dog. To correct this the handler should take hold of the leash near the clip with the left hand with thumb on the top, bend down at the knees, say 'Heel!' and jerk back firmly and horizontally, i.e. at the dog's shoulder height (**Fig. 71**). If the handler takes hold of the leash the other way, whereby it is coming from the little finger towards the dog's collar, and gives a firm jerk, then it becomes a huge strain on the little finger which will become very sore. If the leash is jerked backwards and upwards at the same time, say at 45°, then about half of the handler's energy is being wasted in trying to lift the dog up off the ground (**Fig. 72**). If the handler bends forward from the waist, his or her body weight is toppling forwards and the handler is likely to be dragged forward. But by bending at

Fig. 72. When carrying out this correction, do not jerk up and back at 45° as you will be wasting about half your energy in trying to lift the dog off the ground. Note that the further up the leash you take hold of it, the more difficult it is to jerk the dog back accurately to your side and if the leash is held, as shown, a great strain will be put on your little finger.

the knees, the handler's body weight can act backwards and greatly assist when giving the dog a jerk backwards instead of relying entirely on muscle power.

This correction should be given as soon as the dog starts to surge forward. It is also very important that the handler lets go with the left hand immediately the jerk has been given. If it is held tight, even for a second

or more, then tension on the leash will increase and the dog will naturally pull forward against it.

Over the years I have had a few people who have suffered from arthritis in the joints of their hands. I very much appreciate how painful this is and therefore know how difficult it is for them to grip a leash to give a correction like this. So my advice to anyone who suffers from arthritis or any other ailment is not to choose a large, strong dog which you cannot control.

I have also had some young to middle-aged women who complain that it hurts when they grip a leash like this because their long finger nails dig into their hands! My answer to that problem is, 'Might I suggest that you cut your finger nails!'.

The correct use of your hands can make training very easy and your dog will learn quickly, but if they are used incorrectly, all sorts of problems can occur. Take for example the sit exercise. You should keep your eyes on your right hand, which holds the leash near the clip, and ensure that it is held upright at 90°. Feel only with your left hand, with thumb facing to the left, as you push the dog's hindquarters downwards and forwards, bringing its hind feet up to its forepaws (**Figs 73, 74, 75** and **76**). This action is just like throwing a cricket ball underarm. The common fault that occurs is where handlers pull the leash back and up at about 45° while they push the dog's hindquarters downwards and forwards with the left hand. The dog feels that it is being tossed over on to its back which it naturally resents and in consequence resists or sits crook-

Fig. 73. *Teaching the dog to sit correctly*
In preparation hold the leash near the clip in your right hand vertically above the dog's head and place your left hand over the dog's hindquarters. Note that the dog's front paws are just behind the white line.

Fig. 74. Command the dog to 'Sit' and push downwards and forwards bringing its hindquarters up to its front paws which have not moved.

edly. Another common fault is where handlers push their dog's hindquarters straight down with their thumbs facing towards them. In doing this, they tend to squeeze their dogs in the kidney region which is unpleasant and the dog's front paws retreat to the dog's hind feet, which makes the dog sit too far back. Another fault which is often seen in training dogs to sit is that instead of the handlers keeping their body weight over their feet by bending at their knees and keeping their feet facing straight when they push their dogs down, they bend from the waist and turn their feet in towards

and sometimes under the dog. Naturally the dog sits away to the left. So collectively all these faults, including clumsy footwork, can cause some real problems (**Fig. 77**).

When you come home and bend down to greet your puppy, it associates you bending down to mean 'Come'. Thus it is important that when you teach your dog to 'Stay', you keep upright. So often a puppy or young dog has looked like moving and the handler has bent down and said 'Stay'. In nearly every case the dog has moved. You can readily see why the dog moves and is confused. The hand-

Fig. 75. It is important to hold the leash up at 90°, spread your left hand around the dog's hindquarters with thumb facing to the left and keep your feet facing straight.

Fig. 76. Having praised the dog for sitting, wait a few seconds and dismiss the dog by saying 'Go free', using a simultaneous hand signal with both hands in a slow sweeping manner so that it understands that the lesson has finished.

ler is telling the dog to remain there, but although not realising at the time, he or she is actually signalling by bending down and leaning slightly forwards for the dog to come. So the point to remember when you are teaching stays is to keep upright and by doing this you will also get the dog to look up at you as you make the most of your height.

Many handlers have co-ordination difficulties and usually they are the first to admit it. The reasons why are difficult to understand but most, if not all, go back to childhood. The question is, can they be overcome and how? Once again I believe in the vast majority of cases they can. For example, take the left turn, where you have to say 'Heel!', jerk back on the leash, at the dog's shoulder height, spin on the ball of your left foot and swing your right foot around and across in front of the dog and keep walking. It all seems quite logical and straight forward, but for many it is hard for them to co-ordinate all these actions to achieve success.

When this difficulty arises I tell the handler not to worry as I have another way which should help, and further demonstrate, without a dog, just the

Fig. 77. *The incorrect way of sitting a dog*
This dog was standing just behind the line as in Fig. 73. The common faults which handlers make are pulling the leash back and up at about 45° and also to the left, turning towards and stepping into the dog, placing the left hand with thumb facing to the right and possibly giving the command 'Sit' after this action.

The result is that the dog sits back, crooked, away to the left, its hindquarters often flop to one side and the dog becomes afraid of being stepped into.

footwork alone as I walk around in a small square. I then hold the handler's dog while he or she walks around in a small square. When the handler has mastered the footwork, I then ask him or her to do it again, saying 'Heel!' and giving the imaginary dog a horizontal backward jerk with an imaginary leash in the left hand. When the handler has got this right I hand the

dog back and ask him or her to try doing it with the dog. This is done and often with great accuracy. It is also most gratifying for the handler to know that what at first seemed to be a co-ordination difficulty has finally been overcome.

When I was doing my basic training in the Royal Air Force I saw a number of men who had bad co-ordination, but with constant training and determination they overcame their difficulties. However, I well remember one man who could not walk naturally with alternate arms and legs swinging together. Instead, his left arm went forward as his left foot stepped forward, and the same with his right limbs. The instructors did all they could to help him, but to no avail. Academically he was very clever and by profession he was a solicitor. Regrettably he had to accept that he could not march in the training squadron, but just had to walk on his own.

Perhaps the worst fault created by handlers' total body movement is seen in the recall where, having called their dogs, they suddenly lunge to grab them with one or both hands! Dogs soon come to learn that when they get within a metre or so of their handlers, they are going to be pounced upon. Is it any wonder then that these dogs then fly off at a tangent?

First of all this problem and the cause of this problem needs to be explained to the handlers and the reason why their dogs run off again. The next thing to do is to constantly remind them to keep their hands together, in front of them, as if they were handcuffed! At the same time they should walk slowly backwards encouraging

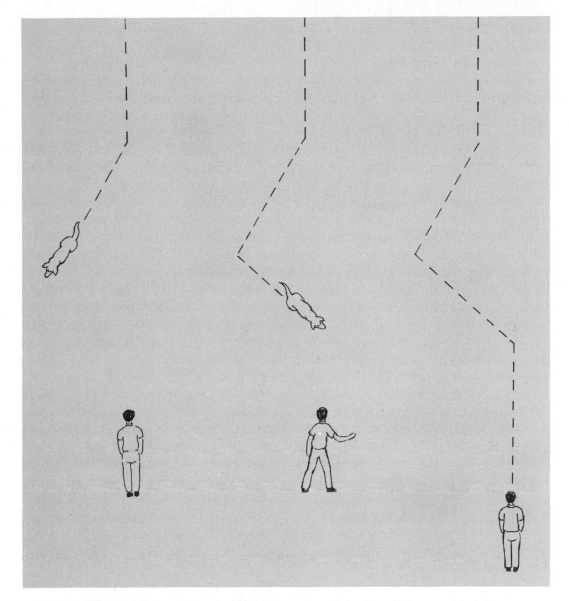

Fig. 78. (a) The handler calls the dog which comes straight then deviates to its right.
(b) As soon as this fault occurs the handler should lean and step wide in the opposite direction, calling the dog.
(c) As the dog comes over to the front of the handler, the handler walks backwards in a line parallel to what he was on originally and the dog comes in straight to sit in front of him.

their dogs to come in straight to sit, so that in time these dogs will come to learn that they are loving, rewarding hands and not the grabbing ones they once wanted to avoid.

A major fault made by the handler's incorrect body position is also seen in the recall. This is where the handler sees the dog coming, but over to one side or the other, and moves over in that direction in order to meet the dog. This is very bad, because the dog will then assume that when it is called the handler will side step a few paces to meet it. This can easily be corrected, however, by getting the handler to move sideways in the opposite direction, encouraging and guiding the dog to come to him or her. This is the correct way by which the handler can make full use of changing body position (**Fig. 78**).

Naturally the people most handicapped with physical problems are the disabled, and instructors should give greater assistance to help them achieve success with their dogs. Depending upon the disability, instructors should also try to work out the best way whereby the disabled person can control his or her dog.

If the person has lost his or her left arm or it is immobilised in any way, then obviously the best thing to do is for the dog to be trained to heel on the right. This can also apply to a person who has had a back injury which somehow affects the left arm. When training and working a dog on the right, the slip-chain collar must be put on the opposite way to when a dog is on the left.

Handlers in wheeled chairs naturally have a few problems, but these can usually be overcome. One young lady who recently sought my help, explained that the only problem she had was when she tried to turn left in heelwork. The dog was not quick enough to see the wheel chair turn and in consequence it became very cautious of being accidentally bumped.

Fortunately the dog knew the command to 'Stand', so I told her to say just that, then turn the chair to the left and say 'Heel'. This worked extremely well and the dog's confidence was restored. By doing everything slowly like this, the dog was able to learn to slow up and turn when it saw the wheeled chair turn.

It is interesting to note that although a disabled person is physically handicapped, his or her determination to succeed is often greater than that of people who are not so afflicted. And another interesting thing is that the dogs which belong to disabled people often seem to understand their owners' limitations and become quite gentle. Uncanny as it may seem, they just have a way of knowing.

16 Your Character

It is often said that as a dog grows up its temperament reflects that of its owner. This is true in many cases, and funnily enough some people get to look like their dogs, and if they don't look like them they act like them, and what they often wear somehow seems to tone in with the dog's appearance!

The owner's temperament can have a great bearing on his or her dog. A very calm, easy-going person will often have a quiet, relaxed dog. But a person who has a somewhat aggressive nature or who is tense and under a lot of pressure is quite likely to have a dog which is on edge and borders on being aggressive.

Over the years I have noticed that people in the country are very relaxed and so are their dogs. They have very few problems and when they take up dog training they sail through quite happily. But people who live in fast moving and busy cities seem to get caught up in the rat race of life; they tend to transmit this to their dogs and problems emerge.

I have said for a long time now that you must always have a very positive attitude when you take up dog train-ing, or any other form of training for that matter. It is no good saying. 'I don't think I'll be able to train the dog!' or 'I know it won't obey me!' Make up your mind you are going to do it, and you will do it. It doesn't matter how long it takes, or what methods you might have to use. Be determined, get on with the job, enjoy what you are doing and in a very short time you and your dog will be working happily together. If things go wrong, don't worry, try again, you will get there. Don't brood over the bad things that your dog does, but cherish the good things about it.

Some people have what we call a natural ability to understand and read dogs, especially if they have been raised with them from the time they were born. But it does not mean to say that people who have not had that opportunity early in life, cannot achieve the same level of success. Believe it or not, they can and do. There are many people who had no idea that they had that hidden ability to train dogs, while others seem to under-estimate their abilities.

As I have said before, when people

come for their first training lesson with their dogs, it is not until about half-way through the lesson that they suddenly realise that they have more to learn than their dogs, and they also admit that they have made many mistakes with their dogs in the past. It is very good when they do admit this. After a while they will further admit that by nature they are nervous, shy, lazy, soft-hearted, impatient, excitable, or have any one of a variety of shortcomings. Some will openly admit that they find it hard to remember things in training, while others will confess that they find it hard to understand a dog.

There are a few whom you find out, sooner or later, have an aggressive streak in their nature. And there are some who are defeatists and lack in confidence and determination. Seldom do I meet the 'know-all' type of person, but they do exist and they are the type who are always ready to blame the dog if anything goes wrong!

So you see, there are just as many different types of temperament in people as there are seemingly in dogs. And this is yet another reason why problems arise. What instructors have to do is to tactfully steer these people in the right direction in training and handling their dogs, always trying to prevent problems starting and correcting ones which are already there.

Calm people who have a good positive attitude rarely seem to have any real problems except that possibly some might become a little complacent after a time and this could be a time when some dogs might take advantage. However, if they are forewarned, they should be able to cope quite easily if such occasions arise. But aggressive people need to be handled with care. They need to be shown how to really love and value their dogs and, in so doing, will be rewarded with affection and responses of great willingness from their dogs.

Those who have a negative attitude need to be politely and firmly told to snap out of it. Whenever I have shown handlers what to do and handed them the leash and invited them to have a go and they have said, 'Oh! I know I'll never be able to do it!' I have pulled them up quickly and said, 'Never, never say that. I want to hear you say, "Great! Let me have a go, I'm going to do it myself", then get on with it.' When they are told this it is not long before they develop a more positive attitude, especially when they get good results.

Nervous people need a lot of support, reassurance and praise for their efforts. Some forms of nervousness are so bad that handlers can be seen to physically shake. In cases such as these it is a good idea to take the handlers with their dogs for a long, steady walk in a quiet area, and if the instructor talks in a quiet, slow and reassuring manner and does not give too many instructions, it is surprising how well they start to relax. When they are relaxed they are able to absorb much more training and convey their calmness to their dogs.

A few people are shy at first and feel embarrassed about using their voices when training their dogs. This is where the instructor has to use his or her voice to encourage them to use theirs. You see a lot of this in beginner classes at obedience dog clubs and I

132

always think it is good when one or two experienced people can work their dogs in these classes. The new people hear them use their voices and in quite a short time you will see how infectious it becomes as they all start talking to their dogs. This is a tremendous help to the instructor who is taking the class.

A lot of people will openly admit they are soft-hearted with their dogs, with the result that their dogs, particularly the clever ones, get away with more or less everything. You will nearly always find that these people most certainly have a very strong and loving affection for their dogs and this is something which I believe instructors should credit them with. But, at the same time, handlers must understand that they have got to be firm and consistent with everything they do with their dogs if they wish to achieve success.

A few people are impatient, and they have to be slowed down in a way. I always quote the proverb, 'Rome wasn't built in a day', to impatient people, and go on to tell them that they must give it time, not to expect too much from their dogs and that very soon they will understand that if they are patient they will achieve success sometimes earlier than they had ever imagined.

Excitable people need to be calmed down in the way they speak and the way they move around when training their dogs. I shall always remember a man in a dog club in England at which I regularly instructed years ago. When it came to teaching the class to do a sit-stay exercise on the leash with their dogs, he would say 'Stay' in a

very excitable voice and move so quickly with shuffling footsteps to get around in front of his dog. All this naturally excited the dog, who repeatedly got up. So I went over to him and said in a very quiet and slow voice, 'Let's try again, Sir! Just say "Stay" once in a firm but quiet voice and then step around in front of the dog very slowly indeed, and move very slowly when you return to the dog.' By talking to the man very slowly this had the calming effect on him. Then he in turn had a calming effect on his dog. All this worked out extremely well over the few months he attended the club. But the interesting thing was that when we had our Christmas party (the dogs were left at home that night), during the course of the social gathering, his wife told me how much more relaxed her husband had become at home since he had been coming for training with their Dalmatian to our club every week. I remember her saying, 'My husband seems a different man. He is so much more relaxed now, whereas before he came here with the dog, he was very tense and excited with anything he did. I'm sure the dog training, which he really enjoys, has helped him in this way!' I was so glad to hear her remarks and said that I was quite sure that she was right. It is so nice to hear stories like this, isn't it? I always think it makes you realise how worthwhile the job has been and what an important role the dog has played in the life of his owner.

Quite a large number of people have a lapse of memory for a number of points in dog training, even to the point of worrying about them. I have always found it best when training these people, who have a genuine difficulty in trying to remember everything, to tell them not to worry and that we will go over those points again. By constantly reminding and preparing them for what they have to do, and by getting them to do things by repetition, they eventually master it. The main point here is to try and prevent people worrying and to praise them up for everything they do well.

You will always find a few people who have a genuine lack of understanding of a dog. You cannot really blame them, because it is similar to any of us who may decide to learn a foreign language or a handy craft of some kind; things with which we have had no real contact before. Therefore it is a case of explaining everything to them in the simplest possible way.

In dog training circles you will always find people who lack confidence and determination and even a few who are defeatists. You will also find that a lot of them will be quite prepared to talk about all their problems, but will not get up and try and do something about them. What we have to do therefore is to get behind them and give them a push, as it were, and say something like, 'Come on, let's give it a go! Let's sort this problem out together because I believe we can do it! On your feet! Bring your dog to heel, and let's get on with the job!'

Fortunately it is very seldom that you find really lazy handlers, because nearly all who want to train their dogs realise they have got to practise a little bit every day. However, it does happen and in nearly all the cases of laziness that I have been in personal contact with, the handlers were young boys. They were usually boys who had been told by their parents that they had to attend training classes with their dogs. Very often they were boys who had not received adequate discipline at home or at school. They showed themselves to be sloppy, inattentive and all they wanted to do was slouch along and chew gum! Personally, I will not tolerate this, and will at the outset ask them to remove their gum while I am training, just as I would ask any handler to kindly refrain from smoking while actually handling a dog. In the past, I have seen many a dog put off by the careless way the handler has gone to stroke the dog, or take a retrieved article from the dog's mouth, while he or she had a lighted cigarette in their hand.

And so when you take a close look at all these different temperamental characteristics in people, you can appreciate how each one can have a particular effect on his or her dog. While most of these pople are aware of their faults, others have to be politely told how they are affecting their dogs. After this it is a case of guiding them in the most appropriate ways to correct those faults and to try and prevent others developing. Finally, after all the hard work the handlers have put in to train their dogs, I believe it is so important to share in their enjoyment of success, no matter how great or small it is.

17 Your Attire

Who would ever have thought that some of the things you wear, whether they be articles of clothing or trinkets, could affect your dogs and cause problems. But believe it or not, they can, and the dogs which are normally affected are those with some form of suspicion or a high hearing or body sensitivity.

When handling, training and showing dogs it is always best to wear clothing which is comfortable and fairly close-fitting, and footwear should be comfortable and flat, with a secure fitting so that you have a good balance and a good grip on the ground.

Although these points are mentioned to dog owners before they come for training, many of them either forget or do not regard them as being very important. But they soon find out that this advice has been given for their benefit and to prevent any problems arising with their dogs.

A wide dress or wide, light raincoat can so easily flap in the wind and disturb a small to medium-sized dog and cause it to walk wide instead of close to heel. Furthermore, it is difficult for a lady to watch her little dog if it be- comes hidden from view under such a large garment. So therefore, the best thing she can do is to wear slacks. They are ideal and the various modern designs look very smart.

In wet weather some people wear nylon waterproof overtrousers for protection. These are very good, but the particular noise they make as the handler walks along can affect the dog, if it has a very high hearing sensitivity, and it is therefore likely to walk wide.

Rarely are steel tips worn on shoes these days, but I can remember in the fifties and sixties they were, and this affected a number of dogs with high hearing sensitivity as they walked on concrete, tarmac footpaths or wooden floors. I first had this brought to my attention when I was training guide dogs. As trainers we always wore rubber soles and heels, but many of the blind people who came to train with guide dogs wore steel tips on their shoes and in no time at all the sensitive dogs started to walk wide. As soon as these were changed to rubbers, the dogs were at ease again and walked close to their owners whom they were guiding.

Sandals are not ideal as they do not give you the support and grip on the ground that you need, especially when you are training a powerful dog. Thongs are even worse and you will walk out of these when it is necessary to walk backwards as you have to, for instance, when teaching a dog the recall.

High-heeled shoes or boots should never be worn when training dogs. You can so easily overbalance and have a nasty accident and lose control of the dog. Not only that, I have seen many women lose their balance and accidentally tread on their dogs with their heels, some of which are rather pointed.

It was not long after I set up my own dog training school in 1975 that a young lady came to me with her Samoyed which she wanted to show. While it was a lovely looking dog with a most friendly temperament, it had had no basic obedience training whatsoever, and it pulled tremendously on the leash.

At that time it was fashionable for some people to wear high platform soles on shoes, and bell-bottomed slacks. Now although I had requested her, as I do with all clients when they make their first appointment, not to wear high heeled or platform-soled shoes, etc., she nevertheless arrived wearing these, and bell-bottomed slacks! She soon found out what I had forewarned, as she could not really get a good grip on the ground and had great difficulty in trying to keep her balance. I was forever having to catch her as she continued to be pulled over by her Samoyed.

Anyway, when she arrived for the second lesson the following week, she remembered to bring her sneakers, which she put on as soon as she got out of her car. These running shoes enabled her to have an excellent grip on the ground, but unfortunately she was still wearing her bell-bottomed slacks which draped right over her sneakers, and she was forever tripping up on them. Once again, I was forever having to catch her in case she fell flat on her face. So after a while I asked her if she would mind rolling up her bell-bottomed slacks so that she would not trip up. This she did and what a comical sight she was then! Fortunately, she had a very good sense of humour and we both had a good laugh at the way she looked and the dog joined in with a broad grin on his face! However, we got on with the training and the dog really started to make progress.

When she arrived the next week, I had the surprise of my life as she got her dog out of her car and walked up my driveway wearing a beautiful black dress studded with sequins, and was wearing high heeled shoes to match! I naturally commented on how beautifully dressed she was, whereupon she explained that she came dressed like that because she was going on to a dance that evening! I politely reminded her about her footwear, and as luck would have it, she remembered that she still had her sneakers in the car.

She returned to her car to change her shoes and as it happened a cool breeze sprang up, so she draped an expensive white stole around her shoulders to keep warm. We lost no time in getting on with some heelwork, and I was so pleased to see how well her Samoyed was heeling. She had obviously been working on him throughout the week. However, her stole kept on fluttering in his face and this caused him to walk wide and sometimes sit wide. So once again, I had to point out why he was doing this and asked her if she would mind putting her stole back in her car. She understood this of course and had a little chuckle to herself and said that she wondered if she would ever wear the right clothes for training!

Well, when she came for her fourth lesson she had obviously put a lot of thought into what she would wear. She wore well tailored close fitting slacks with sweater to match and a good pair of flat, laced-up shoes. Soon after we started training, and by that time she was doing recalls on the leash, I noticed that a large, heavy bonze medallion which hung low around her neck kept swinging on to the dog's nose every time she had to lean over to sit or praise her dog. Any trinket like that swinging on to a dog's face will surely disturb him and he will then keep away. So I had to ask her if she would mind removing it or dropping it down inside her sweater.

I wondered if I was ever going to win with that girl, but I am glad to say that in subsequent lessons she always came appropriately dressed for training. All this goes to show that you must wear the right type of clothes and footwear and not wear any trinkets like heavy medallions, or even bangles. These can make a lot of noise and, if the dog has a high hearing sensitivity, can put it off. Quite a few times I have asked ladies who have been wearing a lot of bangles on their arms if they would mind removing them while they were training their dogs.

There are so many different things which can put dogs off and I well remember a very beautiful girl who brought her Labrador to me for training. She had very long, well-groomed hair, and every time she bent down to praise her dog the slight wind would blow her hair across her eyes so that she could not see, and at the same time it disturbed her dog so much that he kept moving away. The problem was soon solved! I supplied her with a wide elastic band as part of her training equipment! Securing her hair with this, she found it so much easier for them both to work together.

A mistake which is often made by both men and women when they start doing recalls off the leash is to hang the leash around their necks. When they have called their dogs, which have come and sat in front of them, as they bend over to either praise their dogs or correct any crooked sits, the leashes swing and knock the dogs' noses or faces, and when a heavy clip of a leash does that, it can hurt. So I always advise people to either have their leashes folded up neatly in their hands or in their pockets.

This brings me on to another point when doing these recalls, and other exercises which involve a recall, and that is to ensure that the length of the dogs' slip-chain collars are just large enough to go on to and be taken off their heads. If they are too long, the end will hang down so much that it will knock against the dog's front paws as it comes in. This sort of thing can really deter willing little dogs, who have a high body sensitivity, from doing fast recalls.

Another point about slip-chain collars is that many people attach their dog's registration disc and/or other medallions on the ring to which the leash is fastened. And in addition to this some people also attach another disc to the clip part of the leash. As they walk at heel and possibly have to give the occasional corrective jerk on the leash, this wretched noise of tinkle, tinkle made by these medallions can affect a dog with a high hearing sensitivity and cause it to go wide. So if you wish to have medallions on the slip-chain collar, they can be attached further round the collar so that they hang directly underneath the dog's neck where they are virtually noiseless.

Many dogs, particularly young ones, will show suspicion when they see an approaching stranger wearing a hat and/or sun-glasses. It is always a good idea to remove such things when you meet a strange dog, especially a suspicious one. When it has settled down with you, then replace them and it will feel quite relaxed.

Once again, it is best to take these preventive measures. You don't want to create or worsen any problems.

It is often said that it is the owner who creates the problem. This is very true in the vast majority of cases, but not every time. In recent years I attended an obedience trial which was held on a cold, showery day. One of the judges wore a huge cape-like raincoat, and as she approached each dog to carry out the stand for examination exercise, the wind blew this huge garment so much that it frightened every dog. You could not blame the dogs, they had never been subjected to this sort of thing before. Fortunately, the judge was asked to take it off and the rest of the dogs were all right. I am quite sure that person will not wear that garment again when judging, and I quote this event to show how you must all be very careful, not only when handling your own dogs but when handling others.

Yes, in this business, you really have to try to think like a dog! And when you can you will have a better understanding of how it sees you and everything in the world around it.

18 Conclusion

The problems which I have spoken about seem to be only a few of the many which exist. Literally, volumes and volumes of books could be written on this one subject, the reason being that every dog is different, every owner is different and the circumstances in which both live together are different. But as I have said before, when you examine all these you realise that in the vast majority of cases it is the owners who create the problems, but it is the dog which ultimately suffers.

To overcome these difficulties and prevent the problems, everyone needs to face up to their responsibilties as dog owners. This is not as easy as it sounds, but needs careful thought as to what type of dog they wish to have and manage. They must be prepared to give it the sincere love it deserves and to provide the best for it in its health, conditioning, socialising and training.

It is no good acting on a sympathetic impulse at the moment of seeing little puppies in the window of a pet shop, for instance, and going in to buy one. Think very carefully. Have a good look around first. Read books on dogs, visit various dog shows, watch the variety of dogs being trained at obedience dog clubs, ask experts who know about dogs. Observe your friends' dogs in their home environments. Check out as many things as you can first. The next stage is to visit breeders, observe the temperament of the respective sires and dams, then look closely and for some time at the litters they have produced.

Remember, what you choose will hopefully be the dog which is going to be primarily your companion for, say, the next 12 years. It should not be bought as a present for a small child or any other member of the family, but should be bought as a pet for the home and the whole family should be considered. It is quite wrong to buy a dog for a small child and expect him or her to train, condition and socialise the dog outside as well as in the home environment. All this work should be carried out consistently by older children and adults who can take on this responsible task.

A dog needs to be loved as one of the family, but at the same time it has

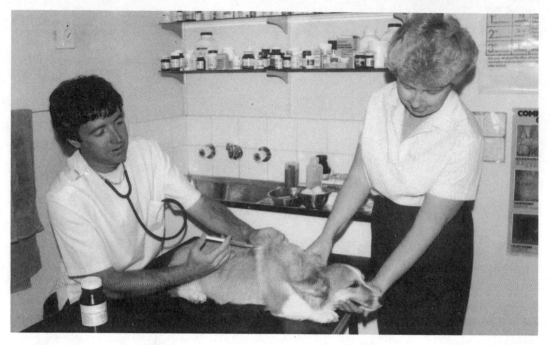

Fig. 79. This little Welsh Corgi was unmanageable and aggressive on the veterinarian's table. After 2 weeks obedience training he was so well behaved that he then liked going to the surgery.

to be taught, as children should be, what is acceptable and what is not. You have to respect your dogs' needs and requirements just as you expect them to respect you as master. You have to be prepared to give much time to your dogs, especially during puppyhood, in getting them out into the community, so that they become conditioned to and well socialised with people, other animals and the multitude of things and activities seen every day.

You need to be constantly aware of your dog's behaviour and as soon as you detect a problem starting to present itself, expert advice should always be sought. It is foolish to delay, as it may prove to be more difficult or even impossible to correct later on.

The same goes for the general health and care of dogs. As soon as you observe something which does not seem right, you should consult a veterinary surgeon. They provide a tremendous service for animals and sometimes I do not think they get the recognition and praise they deserve. Above all, you owe it to your animals to see that they receive the necessary care veterinarians can and do give, and at the same time these highly professional people welcome it when pet owners can get their animals to the surgeries as soon as the illness or ailment is noticed and not several weeks later when they are at death's door. Veterinarians also welcome it when owners have obedience trained their dogs as they have so much more control over them in surgeries (**Fig. 79**).

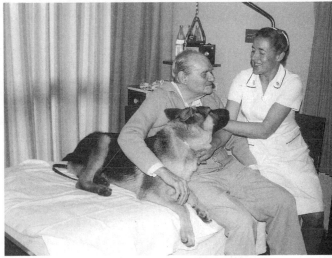

Fig. 80, 81. *Pets as therapy*
This German Shepherd puppy owned and trained by the sister brings much comfort to the patients when he visits them in a Melbourne Nursing Home.

Because of the tremendously high dog population it is highly recommended that dogs and bitches, which are not going to be used for breeding, be desexed. Once again, it is your responsibility to arrange this with your veterinarian. That is one way everyone can play their part in reducing the number of unwanted pregnancies, but it should also be the responsibility of breeders to cut back on breeding, and when they do breed, breed only from the best temperament. It is a very sad thing in many quarters of the breeding and showing world where breeders are absolutely obsessed with breeding dogs to be show winners. Many breeders are lucky in achieving these goals, but a large number of pups which do not shape up to this standard are sold off as pets and this is another reason for the high dog population.

So often you see the greedy person who has the attitude, 'What is in it for me?' Wouldn't it be nicer if we saw more of the attitude, 'What can I do for the other fellow'? It should not therefore be a case of going all out to win at shows, but to be able to produce dogs with good sound temperament and for those puppies to be sold and placed in good homes.

You must be careful not to take on too much. By this I mean you should only take on a dog which you can physically control and not to have two or more which you find difficult to manage.

Responsible dog owners have to be observant, considerate, firm, kind, patient, understanding and give their dogs the credit they deserve. Dogs should be loved and cherished, for apart from being loyal companions they are our guards in many respects such as warning us by barking when people approach our premises or giving some indication of strange things or situations. That is all part of the dog's instinct of self-preservation.

The dog has been a companion and workmate to humans in many fields throughout the centuries. It has been used in various forms of hunting, as a sheep and cattle dog, a retriever in gun-dog work, as a guide dog for the blind, a police dog, messenger dog, casualty-finding dog, avalanche rescue dog, sled dog, and in very recent times the armed services, customs and police forces have trained dogs to detect narcotics and explosives. In the last few years a few charitable organisations have successfully trained hearing dogs for the deaf, service dogs for the disabled and companion dogs which are placed with carefully selected individuals in a program known as Pets As Therapy (PAT).*

PAT dogs are also to be found visiting or residing in nursing homes, special schools and hospitals. Their presence has been highly regarded by members of the medical and nursing professions as these dogs have spread a great deal of happiness and 'healing' as they go about their 'rounds' visiting patients, handing out unconditional love and affection instead of pills (**Figs 80 and 81**).

So enjoy your dogs. A dog can give you so much pleasure and help you relax as you stroll together across the countryside on a beautiful summer's day and perhaps sit on the river bank viewing nature as the quiet waters flow by, or share its company as it lies down and rests its head on your feet as you sit in front of a homely log fire on a cold winter's night. What a wonderful companion the dog is.

---

*The Royal Guide Dogs for the Blind Association of Australia is carrying out this important community service.

Index